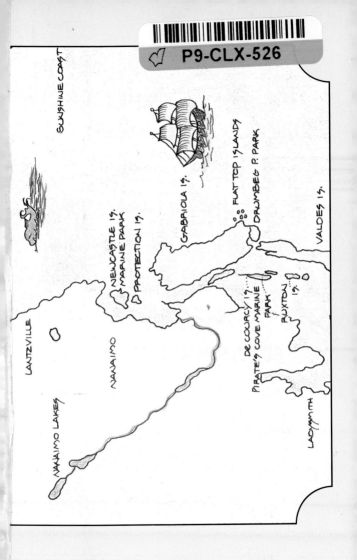

SUNSHINE COAST

LANTZVILLE

NANAIMO LAKES

NANAIMO

NEWCASTLE IS.
MARINE PARK
PROTECTION IS.

GABRIOLA IS.

FLATTOP ISLANDS

DRUMBEG P. PARK

DE COURCY IS.

PIRATE'S COVE MARINE
PARK

RUXTON
IS.

VALDES IS.

LADYSMITH

RAINCOAST POCKET GUIDES

Plants of the
GULF & SAN JUAN ISLANDS
and SOUTHERN VANCOUVER ISLAND

COLLIN VARNER

RAINCOAST BOOKS
Vancouver

Raincoast Books acknowledges the ongoing financial support of the
Government of Canada through The Canada Council for the Arts and
the Book Publishing Industry Development Program (BPIDP); and the
Government of British Columbia through the BC Arts Council.

Edited by Simone Doust
Series design by Ingrid Paulson
Layout by Teresa Bubela

National Library of Canada Cataloguing in Publication Data
Varner, Collin
 Plants of the Gulf and San Juan Islands and Southern Vancouver
 Island / Collin Varner.

 (Raincoast pocket guides)
 Includes bibliographical references and index.
 ISBN 1-55192-604-0

 1. Botany–British Columbia–Gulf Islands. 2. Botany–British
Columbia–Vancouver Island. 3. Botany–Washington (State)–San Juan
Islands. I. Title. II. Series.
QK203.B7V36 2003   581.9711'2   C2002-911416-0

Library of Congress Catalogue Number: 2002096019

Raincoast Books   *In the United States:*
9050 Shaughnessy Street   Publishers Group West
Vancouver, British Columbia   1700 Fourth Street
Canada   V6P 6E5   Berkeley, California
www.raincoast.com   94710

Printed in Hong Kong, China by Book Art Inc., Toronto

10 9 8 7 6 5 4 3 2 1

TABLE OF CONTENTS

British Columbia's Gulf Islands and southern Vancouver Island and Washington State's San Juan Islands offer the ideal getaway for hikers, kayakers and boaters. The hundreds of protected provincial and state marine parks allow the plant explorer a peek into our precious living museums.

The absence of high mountain ranges means that the marine climate surrounding these islands is quite different from that of the adjacent mainlands. With the exception of a handful of smaller mountains, most of the islands consist of rolling hills, high cliffs, meadows and beaches.

Mild, wet winters and dry summers allow a diverse growing range for plant life. Meadows and forests left moist by winter provide ideal spring growing conditions for plants to flower and set seed. The succession of coastal blooms in spring rivals the subalpine meadows of Mount Rainier and the Whistler-Blackcomb region: The colours begin with spring gold and fawn lily, continue with western buttercup, paintbrush, blue-eyed Mary, shooting star, camas, chocolate lily, stonecrop, gum weed and Hooker's onion, and carry into mid-June with the exquisite yellow-flowering prickly-pear cactus.

These flowers decorate the shore-lines, but within the forests another show of colours flares. Salmonberry and Indian plum are usually first to bloom, followed by thimbleberry, false Solomon's seal, fairyslipper,

< Pylades Trail, De Courcy Island

western coralroot, heart-leafed twayblade, fringecup and foam flower. By midsummer, however, the meadow plants have faded away, the grass has turned golden brown and the soil is brick dry.

This guide describes over 150 of the more than 500 vascular plants discovered on the Gulf and San Juan islands. Each species has a fact sheet with three or four entries. DESCRIPTION presents the plant and how to identify it, while HABITAT explains where it grows best. Plants valued by First Nations peoples have an entry for NATIVE USE. In the LOCAL SITES section, I have listed a few places on the islands where each plant can be found and its flowering time. Most of the place names in the LOCAL SITES entries can be found in the maps on the front and back flaps.

Please note that I have included only native plants and introduced species that survive and thrive in the wild. Also note that, to keep the book pocket-sized, I have not included every known species and have been selective with the information given for each cited plant. The observer with a keen interest and a sharp eye can expect to discover more treasures.

— Collin Varner

Paddling through a kelp bed off Drumbeg Park, Gabriola Island

ACKNOWLEDGEMENTS

This guide could not have been completed without the help of many people. I would like to acknowledge and thank the following:

Harvey Janszen, for his plant checklist and careful proofreading.

David Sutherland, Garth Ramsey and Ken Holland, for the many pleasurable months on their sailboats exploring the islands.

My adventurous kayaking partner, Holly Varner.

Katherine Gibson, for putting us up many times at her Gulf Island retreat.

The University of British Columbia, for its support.

British Columbia and Washington State parks staff for their stewardship of our precious natural resources.

The great staff at Raincoast Books: Scott Steedman, Simone Doust, Ingrid Paulson, Teresa Bubela and Marjolein Visser.

Finally, my favourite hiking partner, Wendy.

TWINFLOWER

Linnaea borealis • Honeysuckle family: *Caprifoliaceae*

■ DESCRIPTION Twinflower is an attractive trailing evergreen to 10 cm in height. Its nodding pink flowers are fragrant, to 5 mm long, and borne in pairs at the end of slender, Y-shaped stems. The evergreen leaves are 1 cm long, oval, shiny dark green above and paler below, with minute teeth on the upper half. The genus *Linnaea* is named for Carolus Linnaeus, Swedish botanist and founder of the binomial system for plant and animal classification. Twinflower is said to have been his favourite flower.

■ HABITAT Common in low to mid elevation forests across Canada.

■ LOCAL SITES Common on the mossy forest floors of most islands. Flowers June through July.

< *Helliwell Provincial Park, Hornby Island*

CLIMBING HONEYSUCKLE
Lonicera ciliosa • Honeysuckle family: *Caprifoliaceae*

■ **DESCRIPTION** Climbing honeysuckle is a deciduous woody vine capable of climbing trees to 8 m in height. Its orange flowers are trumpet-shaped, to 4 cm long, and form in clusters in the terminal leaves. By late summer bunches of bright red berries are produced in the cup-shaped leaves. The leaves are oval, 5-8 cm long and, like all honeysuckles, opposite. This species is the showiest of the native honeysuckles. Its main pollinators are hummingbirds and moths. CAUTION: the berries are considered poisonous.

■ **HABITAT** Scattered in low-elevation Douglas fir forests, more common near the ocean and in the Gulf and San Juan islands.

■ **NATIVE USE** The vines were used to weave mats, blankets and bags.

■ **LOCAL SITES** Common on most islands. Flowers from the end of May to June.

HAIRY HONEYSUCKLE or PURPLE HONEYSUCKLE
Lonicera hispidula • Honeysuckle family: *Caprifoliaceae*

■ **DESCRIPTION** Purple honeysuckle is a crawling vine to 4 m long. Its pinkish purple flowers grow to 2 cm long and develop bright red berries by the end of summer. The leaves are similar to those of the climbing honeysuckle: opposite, with the top pair fused to form a cup. The young stems and leaves are lightly haired.

CAUTION: the berries are poisonous.

■ **HABITAT** Dry coniferous forests on southern Vancouver Island, Gulf Islands and San Juan Islands.

■ **LOCAL SITES** Common; good concentrations at Dionisio Point on Galiano Island and Mount Constitution on Orcas Island.

CANADA THISTLE
Cirsium arvense • Aster family: *Asteraceae*

■ DESCRIPTION Canada thistle is an armed herbaceous perennial from 0.7 to 1.5 m in height. Its flowers are more abundant than the bull thistle's (*C. vulgare*) but are smaller (1 cm across) and a lighter shade of purple. Canada thistle is dioecious, meaning the male and female flowers grow on separate plants. The irregularly shaped leaves are green on top, white and hairy beneath and have spiny edges; this thistle does not have spiny wings on its stems. Despite its name, Canada thistle is a native of Europe. The species name *arvense* means "of cultivated fields."

■ HABITAT Common on wasteland and in cultivated areas, at low to mid levels.

■ LOCAL SITES Abundant on most islands. Flowers with bull thistle mid-July through August.

BULL THISTLE

Cirsium vulgare • Aster family: *Asteraceae*

■ **DESCRIPTION** Bull thistle is an introduced, well-armed biennial to 1.7 m in height. Its showy flowers are pinkish purple, well-armed toward the base, to 4 cm long. The leaves are alternate, deeply incised and armed on both the edges and the top surface. This species puts out vegetative growth in the first year and flowers in the second. The species name *vulgare* means "common."

■ **HABITAT** Disturbed sites. Because grazing animals do not eat these plants, they have spread well into fertile pastures and fields.

■ **LOCAL SITES** Common on most islands. Flowers mid-July through August.

WALL LETTUCE
Lactuca muralis • Aster family: *Asteraceae*

■ **DESCRIPTION** Wall lettuce is an introduced herbaceous biennial to 1.5 m tall. Its tiny yellow flowers, which resemble small dandelions, grow in loose clusters to 25 cm across. The fruit (achenes) are small and covered with fluffy hairs. Leaves are variable in size and shape, though most are deeply incised and clasp the stem. The milky sap gave the plant its genus name, *Lactuca*, from the Latin word for milk, *lac*.

16

■ **HABITAT** Very common in southern B.C., on roadsides and highway medians and in open forests.

■ **LOCAL SITES** Common on most islands; found on roadsides and at forest edges.

Flowering starts in June and tapers out in September.

OXEYE DAISY

Chrysanthemum leucanthemum • Aster family: *Asteraceae*

■ **DESCRIPTION** Oxeye daisy is an aromatic herbaceous perennial to 75 cm tall. Its flowers have the typical daisy white ray petals and yellow centre disks, to 5 cm across. The basal leaves are obovate with rounded teeth; the stem leaves are similar, though alternate. This is a European introduction that has naturalized in most of the Pacific Northwest. "Chrysanthemum" is from the Greek *chrysos* ("gold") and *anthos* ("flower").

17

■ **HABITAT** Fields, meadows, very common on roadsides.
■ **LOCAL SITES** Common on the larger islands.
Flowers abundantly from June to August.

GUM WEED
Grindelia integrifolia • Aster family: *Asteraceae*

■ **DESCRIPTION** Gum weed is a herbaceous perennial to 1 m in height. Its yellow ray flowers grow to 5 cm across, with the bracts covered in a gummy latex. The basal leaves are yellowish green, 5-30 cm long and lance-shaped. Gum weeds are halophytes — they need salt, which they get from salt spray from the ocean.

■ **HABITAT** Coastal bluffs, grassy slopes, beaches and saltwater flats.

■ **NATIVE USE** The latex was used to treat asthma, bronchitis and whooping cough.

■ **LOCAL SITES** One of the most common and welcome flowers on the islands. Flower prolifically from June to September.

COMMON TANSY

Tanacetum vulgare • Aster family: *Asteraceae*

■ **DESCRIPTION** Common tansy is an aromatic herbaceous perennial to 1.2 m in height. Its yellow, button-like flowers are grouped together to form attractive flat clusters 5 -10 cm across. The delicate leaves are alternate, finely divided, 5 -25 cm long and up to 10 cm wide. The entire plant has a strong, distinctive scent. Common tansy is a European introduction that has naturalized very well here. It has a long and colourful history, and is still used medicinally and as a culinary flavouring.

■ **HABITAT** Well-drained sites at low elevations.

■ **LOCAL SITES** Scattered on the San Juan Islands, with large concentrations on Saltspring and Hornby islands. A wonderful sight when in full bloom, mid-July to mid-August.

CANADA GOLDENROD
Solidago canadensis • Aster family: *Asteraceae*

■ **DESCRIPTION** Canada goldenrod is a herbaceous perennial of various heights, from 30 to 150 cm. Its small golden flowers are densely packed to form terminal pyramidal clusters. The many small leaves grow at the base of the flowers; they are alternate, lance-linear, sharply saw-toothed to smooth.

■ **HABITAT** Roadsides, wasteland, forest edges at low to mid elevations.

■ **LOCAL SITES** Common on the larger islands. Flowers July and August.

YARROW
Achillea millefolium • Aster family: *Asteraceae*

■ **DESCRIPTION** Yarrow is a herbaceous perennial to 1 m in height. Its many small white flowers form flat-topped clusters 5-10 cm across. The aromatic leaves are so finely dissected that they appear fern-like, hence its species name, "a thousand leaves." The genus is named after Achilles, a hero of Greek mythology.

■ **HABITAT** Roadsides, wasteland, common at low to mid elevations.

■ **NATIVE USE** Infusions and poultices were made for cold remedies.

■ **LOCAL SITES** Widespread on most islands from the seashore to the top of Mount Constitution on Orcas Island and Mount Maxwell on Saltspring Island. Flowers June, July and August.

PEARLY EVERLASTING

Anaphalis margaritacea • Aster family: *Asteraceae*

■ **DESCRIPTION** Pearly everlasting grows to 80 cm in height and produces heads of small yellowish flowers surrounded by dry white bracts. The leaves are lance-shaped, green above and covered with a white felt underneath. If picked before they go to seed, the flowers remain fresh-looking long after they are brought in.

■ **HABITAT** Common on disturbed sites, roadsides and rock outcrops.

22

■ **LOCAL SITES** Common on roadsides and in fields. The flowers can be seen into early winter, well after most other wildflowers are gone. Flowers July and August to September.

PERENNIAL SOW-THISTLE
Sonchus arvensis • Aster family: *Asteraceae*

■ DESCRIPTION Perennial sow-thistle is an introduced herbaceous perennial to 2 m in height. Its yellow flowers, to 5 cm across, resemble large dandelions. The soft-prickled clasping leaves grow to 25 cm long. Three species of sow-thistle are found on the islands, though none are true thistles. Perennial sow-thistle is the largest of these species; prickly sow-thistle (*S. asper*) and common sow-thistle (*S. oleraceus*) are annuals to 1 m in height, with yellow flowers to 1 cm across.

■ HABITAT Roadsides, upper sandy beaches, fields and dry forest edges at low to mid elevations.

■ LOCAL SITES Common; large displays on Orcas, San Juan and Saltspring islands. Flowers June through September and early October.

23

WOOLLY SUNFLOWER or WOOLLY ERIOPHYLLUM
Eriophyllum lanatum • Aster family: *Asteraceae*

■ DESCRIPTION Woolly sunflower is a herbaceous perennial to 60 cm in height. Its bright yellow flowers are borne singly, 3-4 cm across, with 8-11 petals surrounding a centre disc. The woolly leaves to 8 cm long are artemesia green and deeply lobed. The common and genus name *Eriophyllum* refers to the woolly leaves.

■ HABITAT Dry exposed slopes and outcrops at low to mid elevations.

■ LOCAL SITES Common along the coast; good flower displays at Panther Point on Wallace Island and Mount Parke on Mayne Island. Flowers mid-May to July.

OYSTER PLANT or COMMON SALSIFY

Tragopogon porrifolius • Aster family: *Asteraceae*

■ DESCRIPTION Oyster plant is an introduced biennial to 1.2 m in height. Its attractive purple flowers are 4-6 cm across, with bright green bracts protruding beyond the rays; by July and August the flowers turn into large dandelion-like seed heads to 8 cm across. The long grass-like leaves clasp the stems at the base. The species name *porrifolius* means "leaves resembling leeks." The prized fleshy roots are said to taste like oysters.

■ HABITAT Dry roadsides, disturbed sites and meadows.

■ LOCAL SITES Large patches at Montague Harbour on Galiano Island and Beaumont Marine Park on South Pender Island. Flowers end of May through June.

WHITE-FLOWERED HAWKWEED
Hieracium albiflorum • Aster family: *Asteraceae*

■ **DESCRIPTION** White-flowered hawkweed is a herbaceous perennial from 40 cm to 1 m tall. Its creamy white flowers are 1 cm across and, like the dandelion's, the head is made up of only ray flowers. The leaves are mainly basal, lanceolate and hairy. The name "hawkweed" comes from a Greek myth that the juice of the plant would clear the eyes of a hawk.

■ **HABITAT** Disturbed sites, open coniferous forests at low to mid elevations.

■ **LOCAL SITES** Common, flowers June and July at low elevations, August at higher elevations.

TARWEEDS

Madia sp. • Aster family: *Asteraceae*

■ DESCRIPTION There are 6 species of tarweed on the San Juan and Gulf islands, ranging from 15 cm to 1.2 m in height. The small yellow flowers of the tarweed grow 1-2.5 cm across and are comprised of both ray and disc flowers. The leaves are mostly lanceolate and sometimes sticky with a tar scent. Chilean tarweed (*M. sativa*) has an extensive range, growing as far south as Chile. Tarweed is often seen in the same area as white-flowered hawkweed (*Hieracium albiflorum;* see page 26).

■ HABITAT Dry forest edges, open disturbed sites at low elevations.

■ LOCAL SITES Beach trails on most islands. Large concentrations at Campbell Point on Mayne Island and Montague Harbour on Galiano Island.

PATHFINDER
Adenocaulon bicolor • Aster family: *Asteraceae*

■ **DESCRIPTION** Pathfinder is a herbaceous perennial to
1 m tall. Its tiny white flowers are inconspicuous compared
with the large (10-15 cm long) bicoloured, heart-shaped
leaves. The mature seeds are hooked, allowing them to
attach to passing animals and people's clothing. The leaves
flip over when walked through, revealing the silvery
underside and thus marking the path.

28   ■ **HABITAT** Shaded forests at low to mid elevations.
■ **LOCAL SITES** Common in moist forests on larger islands
in moist forests. Flowers June to July.

NODDING ONION

Allium cernuum • Lily family: *Liliaceae*

■ **DESCRIPTION** Nodding onion is a herbaceous perennial, to 45 cm in height. Over a dozen small pink flowers are held in the distinctive nodding umbels. The grassy leaves are basal, to 30 cm long, and similar to those of a green onion. Both bulbs and leaves smell of onion. The species name *cernuum* means "nodding."

■ **HABITAT** Dry grassy slopes, rocky outcrops, forest edges at lower elevations.

■ **NATIVE USE** The cooked onions were a delicacy. In the Salish language, *lillooet* means "place of many onions."

■ **LOCAL SITES** Common on the islands. Jones Island State Marine Park and Isle de Lis are covered in flowers in June and early July, and there are large patches at the top of Mount Constitution on Orcas Island.

HOOKER'S ONION

Allium acuminatum • Lily family: *Liliaceae*

■ **DESCRIPTION** Hooker's onion is a herbaceous perennial to 30 cm in height. Its rose-coloured flowers are held in upright umbels (unlike the nodding onion, *Allium cernuum;* see page 29). The leaves are grass-like and have withered by blooming time. When crushed, the entire plant smells like onion. The species name *acuminatum* refers to the tapering flower petals.

■ **HABITAT** Dry grassy slopes and crevices at low elevations.

■ **NATIVE USE** The small bulbs were eaten raw or steamed.

■ **LOCAL SITES** Fairly common throughout the islands; good concentrations seen on Isle de Lis and at Oak Bluffs on North Pender Island. Flowers mid-May through June.

HARVEST LILY
Brodiaea coronaria • Lily family: *Liliaceae*

■ **DESCRIPTION** Harvest lily is a herbaceous perennial, to 30 cm in height from corms. Its violet-purple, trumpet-shaped flowers are 4 cm long and grow in clusters of 3-5. The leaves are grass-like and have withered by the time the flowers are noticeable.

■ **HABITAT** Isolated to southeastern Vancouver Island, the Gulf Islands and adjacent mainland. Prefers well-drained grassy slopes.

■ **NATIVE USE** The corms were harvested for winter consumption.

■ **LOCAL SITES** Helliwell Provincial Park on Hornby Island, Jones Island State Marine Park and the grassy slopes at Rosario on Orcas Island are covered with thousands of flowers at the end of June through July. Fool's onion (*B. hyacinthina*) can also be found at Cattle Point on San Juan Island.

TIGER LILY

Lilium columbianum • Lily family: *Liliaceae*

■ DESCRIPTION Tiger lily is an elegant herbaceous perennial to 1.5 m tall. Its drooping flowers go from deep yellow to bright orange. A vigorous plant can have 20 or more flowers. Shortly after the flower buds have opened, the tepals curve backwards to reveal maroon spots and anthers. The leaves are lance-shaped, usually in a whorl and 5-10 cm long.
It is said that he or she who smells a tiger lily will develop freckles.

■ HABITAT Diverse range, including open forests, meadows, rock outcrops and the sides of logging roads, at low to subalpine elevations.

■ NATIVE USE The bulbs were boiled or steamed and eaten.

■ LOCAL SITES Not common, but recorded throughout the islands. Flowers early June to July.

FALSE LILY OF THE VALLEY
Maianthemum dilatatum • Lily family: *Liliaceae*

■ **DESCRIPTION** False lily of the valley is a small herbaceous perennial to 30 cm in height. Its small white flowers appear in April/May, clustered on 5-10 cm spikes. The slightly fragrant flowers are quickly replaced by berries 6 mm across; the berries go through summer a speckled green and brown but turn ruby red by autumn. The dark green leaves are alternate, heart-shaped and slightly twisted, to 10 cm long. The genus name *Maianthemum* is from the Greek *Maios* ("May") and *anthemon* ("blossom").

■ **HABITAT** Moist coastal forests at low elevations.

■ **NATIVE USE** The berries were eaten but not highly regarded.

■ **LOCAL SITES** Common on the larger islands that have cool forests. Also at Tribune Bay on Hornby Island and on Discovery Island. Flowers early May. Berries start showing mid-June.

WESTERN WHITE FAWN LILY

Erythronium oregonum • Lily family: *Liliaceae*

■ **DESCRIPTION** Western white fawn lily is a herbaceous perennial to 25 cm in height. The nodding white flowers are adorned with golden anthers, and the seed takes 5 to 7 years to form a corm and put up its first flower; picking of the flowers has greatly reduced the numbers of this plant. The basal leaves are lance-shaped, to 20 cm long, and mottled white to brown, much like a fawn.

■ **HABITAT** Open forests and rocky outcrops at low elevations.

■ **LOCAL SITES** Large patches at Ruckle Provincial Park on Saltspring Island, at Campbell Point on Mayne Island and on Isle de Lis. Flowers March to mid-May.

CHOCOLATE LILY
Fritillaria lanceolata • Lily family: *Liliaceae*

■ **DESCRIPTION** Chocolate lily is a herbaceous perennial from bulb to 80 cm in height. Its nodding flowers are dark brownish purple with greenish yellow mottlings. Each bell-shaped flower has 6 petals to 3 cm across. The leaves are lanceolate and formed in 1 or 2 whorls of 3-5 leaves. The genus name *Fritillaria* refers to the flower's checkered pattern, reminiscent of old dice boxes. This is one of the islands' most prized spring flowers.

■ **HABITAT** Exposed grassy bluffs and meadows, dry to moist soil, low to mid elevations.

■ **NATIVE USE** The bulbs were boiled or steamed and eaten by most Pacific Northwest peoples.

■ **LOCAL SITES** Common on most islands; huge concentrations on Discovery Island and at Iceberg Point on Lopez Island. Both these areas also have the rare banana yellow form (right photo below). Flowers April to May.

COMMON CAMAS

Camassia quamash • Lily family: *Liliaceae*

■ **DESCRIPTION** Common camas is a herbaceous perennial from bulb to 70 cm in height. It has 6 beautiful blue purple tepals to 4 cm across. The long grass-like leaves are slightly shorter than the flowering stem. Great camas (*C. leichtlinii*) is very similar but taller, to 1.2 m. The best way to distinguish the 2 species is by the tepals of the great camas, which twist around the fruit as they wither.

■ **HABITAT** Moist meadows in spring, dry meadows in summer and on grassy slopes at low elevations.

■ **NATIVE USE** The bulbs were a very important food source. Wars were fought over ownership of certain meadows.

■ **LOCAL SITES** Both species are common on the islands. Tens of thousands flower with chocolate lilies (*Fritillaria lanceolata*) and death camas (*Zygadenus venenosus*) on Discovery Island in mid-May. Flowers mid-April through May.

DEATH CAMAS

Zygadenus venenosus • Lily family: *Liliaceae*

■ **DESCRIPTION** Death camas is a herbaceous perennial, to 50 cm in height from bulb. Its small creamy flowers are 1 cm across and neatly arranged in terminal racemes on stems to 50 cm long. The grass-like leaves are mainly basal, to 30 cm long, and have a deep groove like a keel down the centre. The entire plant is poisonous and when out of flower can be confused with the edible common camas (*Camassia quamash;* see page 37).

CAUTION: the entire plant is poisonous.

■ **HABITAT** Rocky outcrops and grassy slopes at low elevations.

■ **NATIVE USE** The bulbs were mashed and used as arrow poison.

■ **LOCAL SITES** Common; large concentrations on Discovery Island. Flowers April to June.

HOOKER'S FAIRYBELLS
Disporum hookeri • Lily family: *Liliaceae*

■ **DESCRIPTION** Hooker's fairybells is an elegant branching herbaceous perennial to 1 m in height. Its white flowers hang in pairs and sometimes in threes, with the stamens extending beyond the petals: this distinguishes Hooker's fairybells from Smith's fairybells (*D. smithii*), whose stamens do not extend beyond the petals. By August the flowers have been replaced by yellow red berries. The common name commemorates Joseph Hooker (1817-1911), a prominent English botanist.

■ **HABITAT** Cool moist forests at low elevations.

■ **NATIVE USE** The berries were considered poisonous.

■ **LOCAL SITES** Not common, recorded on San Juan Island, Saltspring and North Pender islands. Flowers mid-May to June.

SILVERWEED
Potentilla anserina ssp. *pacifica* • Rose family: *Rosaceae*

■ **DESCRIPTION** Silverweed grows to only 30 cm in height but can take over several hectares in favourable conditions. The yellow flowers are produced singly on a leafless stalk. The compound leaves reach 25 cm in length and have 9-19 toothed leaflets; they are bicoloured, grass green above and felty silver below, hence the common name. Silverweed spreads quickly thanks to its fast-growing stolons, which root at the nodes. The genus name *Potentilla* means "powerful," a reference to its medicinal properties.

■ **HABITAT** Saline marshes, meadows and wet run-off areas near the ocean.

■ **NATIVE USE** The cooked roots were an important food source.

■ **LOCAL SITES** Common on most islands. Flowering starts mid-May, continues through June and July.

LARGE-LEAFED AVENS
Geum macrophyllum • Rose family: *Rosaceae*

■ **DESCRIPTION** Large-leafed avens is a herbaceous perennial to 90 cm in height. Its bright yellow flowers resemble buttercups. They are approximately 6 mm across and are produced singularly or in small clusters. The unique round fruit has bristly bent protruding styles that catch on fur and clothing, an excellent way of dispersing the seed. The irregular-shaped larger leaves are 15-20 cm across, while the stem leaves are smaller and 3-lobed.

■ **HABITAT** Prefers moist soil in open forests and beside pathways, trails and roads at low elevations.

■ **NATIVE USE** The roots were boiled and used medicinally.

■ **LOCAL SITES** Common on most islands. Flowers start at the end of April, are full in May and June and linger into July and August.

SMALL-FLOWERED ALUMROOT
Heuchera micrantha • Saxifrage family: *Saxifragaceae*

■ **DESCRIPTION** Small-flowered alumroot is a perennial to 60 cm in height. Its small white flowers are abundant and held on scapes (stems) up to 60 cm tall. The heart-shaped leaves have long hairy stems and are basal. The leaves are slightly longer than they are broad and distinguish this plant from smooth alumroot (*H. glabra*), which has leaves that are broader than they are long. The name "alumroot" is given because the roots are very astringent.

■ **HABITAT** Cliff faces and stream banks at low to high elevations.

■ **LOCAL SITES** Common on most islands. Cliff faces on Jedediah Island, Tribune Bay on Hornby Island and in Ruckle Provincial Park on Saltspring Island. Flowers mid-May to July.

FRINGECUP

Tellima grandiflora • Saxifrage family: *Saxifragaceae*

■ DESCRIPTION Fringecup is a perennial to 80 cm in
height. Its fringed flowers are greenish, fragrant, 1 cm
long and produced on 60- to 80-cm scapes (stems).
The basal leaves are round to heart-shaped, deeply
notched, 5-8 cm across; the scape leaves are smaller.
When out of flower, fringecup can be confused with
the piggy-back plant.

■ HABITAT Moist, cool forests along the coast.

■ NATIVE USE The plants were crushed and boiled
and the resultant infusion was used to treat sickness.

■ LOCAL SITES Common throughout the islands.
An incredible grove of thousands found in the
middle of Portland Island. Flowers from end of
April to end of June.

FOAM FLOWER
Tiarella trifoliata • Saxifrage family: *Saxifragaceae*

■ **DESCRIPTION** Foam flower is a herbaceous perennial to 50 cm in height. Each wiry stem supports several tiny white flowers. The massed flowers are thought to resemble foam. The trifoliate leaves (to 7 cm across) are all basal except for one, located approximately halfway up the stem; this is good for identification. There is another species of foam flower (*T. trifoliata var. unifoliata*) that is very similar except for its solid leaf.

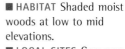

■ **HABITAT** Shaded moist woods at low to mid elevations.
■ **LOCAL SITES** Common in cool forests. Flowers mid-May through July.

PAINTBRUSH
Castilleja sp. • Figwort family: *Scrophulariaceae*

■ **DESCRIPTION** The many species of paintbrush are difficult to distinguish. They range in height from 20 to 80 cm and there is frequent hybridization within their diverse growing range, making identification even harder. Paintbrush is a perennial with small lance-shaped leaves. Its actual flowers are small and inconspicuous — it is the showy red bracts that attract all the attention.

■ **HABITAT** Low-elevation grassy meadows and rocky outcrops to moist subalpine and alpine meadows.

■ **LOCAL SITES** Hairy Indian paintbrush is probably the most common of all the paintbrushes found on the islands. The flower ranges from bright orange to brilliant red and blooms from May to September.

YELLOW MONKEY-FLOWER

Mimulus guttatus • Figwort family: *Scrophulariaceae*

■ **DESCRIPTION** Yellow monkey-flower can be annual
or perennial; normally it self-seeds, disappears and then
germinates as an annual in spring. It can grow to 80 cm
in height. Its beautiful yellow flowers are 2-lipped, to 5 cm
long, with many small and one larger dot on the lower lip.
The lower leaves are oval and grow in pairs, while the
upper leaves hug the stem. Chickweed monkey-flower
(*M. alsinoides*) is smaller, to 20 cm high, and often grows
with the larger variety; its flowers are much smaller and
have only a single dot on the lower lip.

■ **HABITAT** Wet cliffs and ledges at low elevations.

■ **LOCAL SITES** Yellow monkey-flower is common on most
of the islands. Ford Cove on Hornby Island has yellow sheets
of it covering the 7-m cliffs. Chickweed monkey-flower
(*M. alsinoides*) is less common, but has good representation
on Isle de Lis and Gabriola Island. Flowers May to August.

SMALL-FLOWERED BLUE-EYED MARY
Collinsia parviflora • Figwort family: *Scrophulariaceae*

■ DESCRIPTION Small-flowered blue-eyed Mary is a herbaceous perennial 5-30 cm tall. Its flowers are 0.5-1 cm long, white on the upper lips and blue on the bottom. The 1- to 4-cm-long leaves vary in shape from oblong to lanceolate, and the upper leaves form in whorls. Large-flowered blue-eyed Mary (*C. grandiflora*) is similar but has larger flowers (1-1.5 cm). Both species can be seen growing together.

■ HABITAT Open grass-covered rock outcrops at low to mid elevations.

■ LOCAL SITES Common on most of the islands; wonderful spring display is found on Russell and Portland islands. Flowers as early as March, with full colour by April and May.

WILD CARROT or QUEEN ANNE'S LACE
Daucus carota • Carrot family: *Apiaceae*

■ DESCRIPTION Wild carrot is an introduced biennial to 1 m in height. Its small white flowers are grouped together to form showy terminal clusters to 10 cm across. The leaves (to 15 cm long) are dissected to the point that they resemble delicate ferns. If the stems are scratched, a carrot scent is released. Wild carrot and parsnips have long been cultivated in Europe for culinary and medicinal use; records of them date back to 500 B.C.

■ HABITAT Roadsides, abandoned fields and highway medians at low elevations.

■ LOCAL SITES One of the more common weeds on the islands. Very noticeable at the end of July and August when in full flower.

48

WATER-PARSLEY

Oenanthe sarmentosa • Carrot family: *Apiaceae*

■ DESCRIPTION Water-parsley is a semi-aquatic herbaceous perennial to 1 m in height. Its flowers are white, faintly fragrant and borne in flat-topped clusters. The leaves are pinnately divided 2 or 3 times, with deeply toothed leaflets. The overall appearance of the plant is weak and sprawling.

CAUTION: the entire plant is considered poisonous.

■ HABITAT Low-elevation marshes and swamps, occasionally in ditches.

■ LOCAL SITES Common on the larger islands. Flowers mid-June through July.

FINE-LEAFED DESERT PARSLEY or SPRING GOLD
Lomatium utriculatum • Carrot family: *Apiaceae*

■ DESCRIPTION Spring gold is an early-flowering herbaceous perennial 5-30 cm tall. Its tiny conglomerated flowers are a bright canary yellow and held in umbels. The finely dissected leaves resemble a fern or carrot leaf.
■ HABITAT Dry grassy slopes, meadows and outcrops.
■ LOCAL SITES Common; excellent flower displays at Ruckle Provincial Park on Saltspring Island and Iceberg Point on Lopez Island light up bluffs and outcrops in early spring. Has a long flowering period, from mid-March to early June.

PACIFIC SANICLE

Sanicula crassicaulis • Carrot family: *Apiaceae*

■ DESCRIPTION Pacific sanicle is a herbaceous perennial
20 cm - 1 m in height. Its small yellow flowers are held up
in rounded terminal clusters to 1 cm across. The leaves are
mainly basal, palmately lobed, with light venation.

■ HABITAT Dry forests, around rocky outcrops and
beaches.

■ LOCAL SITES Common on most Gulf Islands. Flowers
May and June.

51

MOUNTAIN SWEET CICELY
Osmorhiza chilensis • Carrot family: *Apiaceae*

■ DESCRIPTION Mountain sweet cicely is a herbaceous perennial to 1 m in height. Its thin greenish flowers are small and hard to see in the forest; the thin seeds that develop are brown black and catch easily on socks and other clothing. The leaves are divided into threes, then threes again for a total of 9 leaflets. The licorice-scented root is reputed to have aphrodisiac powers.

■ HABITAT Cool moist forests at low to mid elevations.

■ LOCAL SITES Good concentrations on Wallace Island. Flowers May to June and sets seed very quickly.

COOLEY'S HEDGE-NETTLE
Stachys cooleyae • Mint family: *Lamiaceae*

■ DESCRIPTION Cooley's hedge-nettle is a herbaceous perennial to 1 m in height. Its purply red flowers are trumpet-like with a lower lip; they grow to 4 cm long and are grouped in terminal clusters. The leaves are mint-like with toothed edges, opposite, finely hairy on both sides, to 15 cm long. The stems are square and finely hairy. Cooley's hedge-nettle was first documented in 1891 by Grace Cooley, a professor from New Jersey who saw it near Nanaimo.

53

■ HABITAT Moist open forests and streamsides at low elevations.
■ LOCAL SITES Common on the islands. Discovery Island has large drifts. Flowers mid-June to mid-July.

HEAL-ALL or SELF-HEAL
Prunella vulgaris • Mint family: *Lamiaceae*

■ DESCRIPTION Heal-all is an introduced herbaceous perennial to 40 cm in height. Its purple flowers are 2-lipped, 1-2 cm long, and borne in terminal spikes. The leaves are mostly lance-shaped, opposite, to 7 cm long. The stems are square. As its name suggests, heal-all has long been used medicinally. Seventeenth-century herbalist Nicholas Culpeper prescribed that it be "taken inwardly in syrups for inward wounds, outwardly in unguents and plasters for outward."

■ HABITAT Roadsides, forest edges, fields and parks at low to mid elevations.

■ LOCAL SITES This attractive weed has found its way to most of the inhabited islands and can be seen growing at the forest edges and in lawns. Flowers June through July.

YERBA BUENA
Satureja douglasii • Mint family: *Lamiaceae*

■ DESCRIPTION Yerba buena is a fragrant trailing herbaceous perennial to 1 m long. Its inconspicuous flowers are white or slightly purple and borne in the leaf axils. The egg-shaped leaves grow opposite each other to 3 cm long, are bluntly toothed and scented when crushed. The name yerba buena, meaning "good herb," was given to this plant by missionary Spanish priests in California.

■ HABITAT Dry open forests, mainly associated with southern Vancouver Island, Gulf Islands, San Juan Islands and south.

■ NATIVE USE The leaves were steeped for a refreshing tea.

■ LOCAL SITES Common on most islands. Flowers June to July.

55

WESTERN BUTTERCUP
Ranunculus occidentalis • Buttercup family: *Ranunculaceae*

■ **DESCRIPTION** Western buttercup is a perennial 30-70 cm in height. Its bright yellow flowers to 2.5 cm across have 5 to 8 petals (5 is the norm) half as broad as they are long. The basal leaves are twice divided by 3, with the stem leaves becoming smaller and linear as they progress upwards. Western buttercup often grows with camas and chocolate lily.

■ **HABITAT** Forest edges, moist meadows, coastal bluffs at low to mid elevations.

■ **LOCAL SITES** A common meadow plant on the islands. Flowers April to May.

Aquilegia formosa • Buttercup family: *Ranunculaceae*

■ **DESCRIPTION** Red columbine is a herbaceous perennial to 1 m in height. The drooping red-and-yellow flowers are up to 5 cm across and have 5 scarlet spurs arching backwards; they are almost translucent when the sun shines on them. The leaves are sea green above, paler below, to 8 cm across and twice divided by threes. In the head of the flower is a honey gland that can only be reached by hummingbirds and long-tongued butterflies. The hole that can sometimes be seen above this gland is caused by frustrated bumblebees chewing their way to the nectar. The name "columbine" means "dove," for the five arching spurs said to resemble five doves sitting around a dish.

■ **HABITAT** Moist open forests, meadows and creeksides at low to high elevations.

■ **LOCAL SITES** Mount Constitution on Orcas Island and on Saturna, Mayne, Galiano and Saltspring islands. Flowers June to mid-July.

WESTERN STAR FLOWER
Trientalis latifolia • Primrose family: *Primulaceae*

■ **DESCRIPTION** Western star flower is a small, herbaceous perennial 10-25 cm in height. Its white to pink flowers hang on very thin stalks, making them appear like stars. The oval leaves (5-10 cm long) are elevated in a whorl just under the flower stalks. There is a northern star flower (*T. arctica*) that is confined to bogs and swamps; it is shorter (5-20 cm in height), with white flowers 1.5 cm across and additional leaves on the stem below the whorl of elevated leaves.

■ **HABITAT** Dry to moist coniferous forests at low elevations.

■ **LOCAL SITES** Probably the most abundant forest wildflower on the islands. Forms carpets on Pylades Trail, Pirate's Cove on De Courcy Island. Northern star flower (*T. arctica*) is extensive at Beaverton Marsh on San Juan Island. Flowering begins in June and continues through July.

FIREWEED
Epilobium angustifolium•
Evening primrose family: *Onagraceae*

■ DESCRIPTION Fireweed is a tall herbaceous perennial that reaches heights of 3 m in good soil. Its purply red flowers grow on long, showy terminal clusters. The leaves are alternate, lance-shaped like a willow's, 10-20 cm long and darker green above than below. The minute seeds are produced in pods 5-10 cm long and have silky hairs for easy wind dispersal. Fireweed flowers have long been a

59

beekeeper's favourite. The name "fireweed" comes from the fact that it is one of the first plants to grow on burned sites; typically follows wildfires.

■ HABITAT Common throughout B.C. in open areas and burned sites.

■ NATIVE USE The stem fibres were twisted into twine and made into fishing nets, and the fluffy seeds were used in padding and weaving.

■ LOCAL SITES Common throughout the islands. Flowers June through August.

SKUNK CABBAGE

Lysichiton americanum • Arum family: *Araceae*

■ **DESCRIPTION** Skunk cabbage is a herbaceous perennial to 1.5 m in height and as much as 2 m across. The small greenish flowers are densely packed on a fleshy spike and surrounded by a showy yellow spathe, the emergence of which is a sure sign that spring is near. The tropical-looking leaves can be over 1 m long and 50 cm wide.

■ **HABITAT** Common at low elevations in wet areas such as springs, swamps, seepage areas and floodplains.

■ **NATIVE USE** Skunk cabbage roots were cooked and eaten in spring in times of famine. It is said this poorly named plant has saved the lives of thousands.

■ **LOCAL SITES** Common; extensive patches in low areas in Drumbeg Provincial Park on Gabriola Island. Flowers mid-March to mid-May.

HERB ROBERT
Geranium robertianum • Geranium family: *Geraniaceae*

■ **DESCRIPTION** Herb robert is an introduced, rapid-spreading annual to 45 cm in height. Its flowers (1.5 cm across) range from light pink to reddish purple. The leaves are divided into 3-5 sections and these are divided again. The fruit are pointed capsules to 2 cm long; *geranium* comes from the Greek *geranos* ("crane"), a reference to the beak-like fruit. The dovefoot geranium (*Geranium molle*) has rounded, coarsely toothed leaves and small pink flowers.

■ **HABITAT** Prefers moist, lightly shaded areas at low elevations.

■ **LOCAL SITES** Common on the larger islands; flowers throughout the summer.

VANILLA LEAF
Achlys triphylla • Barberry family: *Berberidaceae*

■ DESCRIPTION Vanilla leaf is a herbaceous perennial to
30 cm in height. Its small white flowers are formed on a
spike that stands above the leaf. The small fruit (achenes)
is crescent-shaped and greenish to reddish purple. The
wavy leaves have long stems and are divided into 3
leaflets, one at each side and the third at the tip. When
dried, the leaves have a faint vanilla-like scent.

■ HABITAT Dry to moist forests at low to mid elevations
in southern B.C.

■ NATIVE USE The
leaves were used as an
insect repellent.

■ LOCAL SITES
Common on the Gulf
Islands. Like a carpet
between Shingle Spit
and Ford Cove on
Hornby Island and
Dionisio Point
Provincial Park on
Galiano Island. Flowers
mid-May to June.

YELLOW FLAG

Iris pseudacorus • Iris family: *Iridaceae*

■ **DESCRIPTION** Yellow flag is a semi-aquatic, herbaceous perennial to 1.2 m in height. Its showy flowers are bright yellow with dark pencilled veins on the lower lips. Each flowering stem usually bears 2 flowers. The leaves are wider (to 4 cm) and taller (to 1.2 m) than most irises. The plant is named after the rainbow goddess Iris for its diversity of flower colours. It is also thought to be the flower symbolized by the fleur-de-lys.

■ **HABITAT** Prefers shallow fresh water, in ditches, ponds and on lakeshores. A European introduction, it has become invasive in some wetland areas.

■ **LOCAL SITES** Naturalized on Orcas, San Juan, Mayne and Galiano islands. Flowers mid-May through June.

WHITE-VEINED WINTERGREEN
or PAINTED WINTERGREEN
Pyrola picta • Heath family: *Ericaceae*

■ DESCRIPTION White-veined wintergreen is an attractive evergreen perennial to 30 cm in height. Its drooping flowers are yellowish green, with a waxy finish; they grow to 1 cm across and have a protruding, curved style. The basal leaves are 5-7 cm long and leathery, dark green with white venation. The species name *picta* means "painted," in reference to the beautiful leaves.

65

■ HABITAT Cool coniferous forests at low to mid elevations.
■ LOCAL SITES Recorded on San Juan Island and on Saturna, Galiano and South Pender islands. Flowers June and July.

PINK WINTERGREEN
Pyrola asarifolia • Heath family: *Ericaceae*

■ **DESCRIPTION** Pink wintergreen is an evergreen perennial to 40 cm in height. Its pinkish flowers, to 1 cm across, are carried on 30- to 40-cm stems. The leaves are roundish to elliptical, 5-8 cm long and formed in a basal rosette. *Pyrola* is from *pyrus* ("pear"), indicating that the leaves are sometimes pear-shaped.

■ **HABITAT** Moist forests with rich soil, where it can form extensive carpets 2 m x 8 m. Low to mid elevations.

■ **LOCAL SITES** Common on Mount Constitution on Orcas Island; also found on Mayne, North and South Pender islands. Flowers June and July.

PRINCE'S PINE

Chimaphila umbellata • Heath family: *Ericaceae*

■ **DESCRIPTION** Prince's pine is a small evergreen shrub to 30 cm in height. The white to pink flowers are waxy, formed in loose nodding clusters held above the foliage; the resulting brownish seed capsules are erect and persist through the winter. The leathery leaves form in whorls, grow to 5 cm long and are sharply toothed.

■ **HABITAT** Cool coniferous forests at low to mid elevations.

■ **NATIVE USE** The leaves were steeped and used as a cold remedy.

■ **LOCAL SITES** Large patches to 3 m by 6 m found trailside at Pirate's Cove on De Courcy Island and on Mount Constitution on Orcas Island.

MENZIES' PIPSISSEWA or LITTLE PRINCE'S PINE
Chimaphila menziesii • Heath family: *Ericaceae*

■ DESCRIPTION Little prince's pine is the daintier of the two *Chimaphila*, reaching a maximum height of only 15 cm. Its creamy-white flowers are slightly fragrant, range from 1-3 per stem and nod above the foliage. The leaves are alternate, to 5 cm long, serrately edged and a darker green than the larger prince's pine (*C. umbellata*). The species is named for Dr. Archibald Menzies, a surgeon and botanist who sailed with Captain George Vancouver.

■ HABITAT Cool coniferous forests at low to mid elevations.

Both species are often found growing in the same area.

■ LOCAL SITES Recorded at higher elevations on Saturna Island and at Mount Constitution on Orcas Island. Flowers June to July.

Plectritis congesta • Valerian family: *Valerianaceae*

■ **DESCRIPTION** Sea blush is a seaside annual to 50 cm
in height. Its small pink flowers are crowded into rounded
terminal clusters. The leaves, 1-4 cm long, are oval and
face opposite each other. The genus and species names
refer to the congested flowers.

■ **HABITAT** Meadows and rock outcrops, from slightly
inland to the ocean.

■ **LOCAL SITES** Abundant on the islands. Can be seen
flowering with fawn lily, camas, blue-eyed Mary and
chocolate lily from
April to June.

BROAD-LEAFED PEAVINE
Lathyrus latifolius • Pea family: *Fabaceae*

■ DESCRIPTION Broad-leafed peavine is a climbing
herbaceous perennial to 2 m long. Its pinkish purple
flowers, to 2.5 cm long, are displayed in loose clusters of
5 to 15. The leaves are opposite, to 14 cm long and 5 cm
wide, and end in curly tendrils. This plant's winged stems
are good for identification. Broad-leafed peavine is an
introduced species from Europe.

70

■ HABITAT Forest edges, roadsides and sandy beaches at
low elevations.

■ LOCAL SITES
Common on the islands
and surrounding areas.
Large concentrations at
Montague Harbour on
Galiano Island. Flowers
June through August.

BEACH PEA
Lathyrus japonicus • Pea family: *Fabaceae*

■ DESCRIPTION Beach pea is a climbing herbaceous perennial to 1.5 m long. Its flowers vary from dark purple to blue and are produced in loose clusters of 2-8. The leaves have 6-12 opposite-facing leaflets, with curly tendrils on the tips. At the bottom of the leaf stem are 2 triangular leaf-like stipules, good identifiers for this species. The small seeds grow in pods 3-7 cm long.

■ HABITAT Sandy beaches, among the logs.

■ NATIVE USE Beach pea seeds were eaten raw or boiled and cured in seal oil.

■ LOCAL SITES
Common beach plant on the islands. Flowers May to July.

71

SMALL HOP-CLOVER
Trifolium dubium • Pea family: *Fabaceae*

■ **DESCRIPTION** Small hop-clover is an introduced annual to 25 cm in height. Its tiny yellow flowers to 6 mm across are formed in rounded clusters. The shamrock-like leaves are trifoliate, to 2 cm long.
■ **HABITAT** Dry slopes, fields and lawns at low elevations.
■ **LOCAL SITES** Has become a weed on most of the islands. Flowers May to July.

ROSE CAMPION

Lychnis coronaria • Pink family: *Caryophyllaceae*

■ DESCRIPTION Rose campion is an introduced perennial
to 1 m in height. Its flowers are velvety red, to 2 cm across,
and held up in open clusters. The leaves are grey with a
light woolly covering, to 10 cm long, reducing in size as
they progress up the stem. Rose campion is a garden
escapee that has invaded most of the Pacific Northwest.
■ HABITAT Dry areas, high beaches, roadsides, disturbed
land at lower elevations.

73

■ LOCAL SITES
Becoming common on
most islands; large
colonies on Orcas and
Galiano islands.
Flowers June and July.

FIELD CHICKWEED
Cerastium arvense • Pink family: *Caryophyllaceae*

■ **DESCRIPTION** Field chickweed is a low-growing perennial to 30 cm in height. Its showy white flowers are 1-1.5 cm across, with 5 deeply notched petals. The leaves are opposite, to 3 cm long, and vary from lanceolate to linear. The species name *arvense* means "field."

■ **HABITAT** Dry areas (especially in spring) on rock bluffs, fields and high beaches.

■ **LOCAL SITES** Common; field chickweed is the dominant white flower seen in meadows and grassy outcrops on the islands in May and June.

SPREADING DOGBANE
Apocynum androsaemifolium •
Dogbane family: *Apocynaceae*

■ **DESCRIPTION** Spreading dogbane is a herbaceous perennial to 80 cm in height. Its pink flowers are bell-shaped, to 0.8 cm long, and hang in beautiful clusters at the branch ends. The egg-shaped leaves are in opposite pairs, to 8 cm long, and droop in hot temperatures. When broken, the red stems exude a milky juice.

■ **HABITAT** Exposd areas, dry forest edges and roadsides at low to high elevations.

■ **NATIVE USE** The stem fibres were used for cordage.

■ **LOCAL SITES** Recorded on Mayne, Saturna, Galiano and Saltspring islands. Also on Mount Constitution on Orcas Island and on San Juan Island. Flowers May, June and July.

SIBERIAN MINER'S LETTUCE
Claytonia sibirica • Purslane family: *Portulacaceae*

■ **DESCRIPTION** Siberian miner's lettuce is a small annual to 30 cm in height. Its small white to pink flowers are 5-petalled and produced in abundance on long, thin, fleshy stems. The basal leaves are long-stemmed, opposite, ovate and, like the stems, succulent. Another species, *C. perfoliata*, (right photo below) differs in that its upper leaves are disc-shaped and fused to other flower stems. Siberian miner's lettuce was first discovered in Russia, where it was a staple food for miners. Early prospectors and settlers found both species made excellent early-season salad greens.

■ **HABITAT** Moist forest areas at low to mid elevations.

■ **LOCAL SITES** Common on the forested islands. Siberian miner's lettuce prefers cool, moist forest floors; miner's lettuce (*C. perfoliata*) grows more in the open.

RATTLESNAKE PLANTAIN
Goodyera oblongifolia • Orchid family: *Orchidaceae*

■ DESCRIPTION Rattlesnake plantain is an evergreen perennial to 40 cm in height. Its numerous small flowers are greenish white, orchid-shaped and produced on a spike 20-40 cm high; they have a tendency to grow on one side of the spike. The evergreen leaves are basal and rosette-like, from 5-10 cm long. They are criss-crossed by whitish veins, creating the rattlesnake pattern that gives the plant its common name.

■ HABITAT Usually found in dry to moist coniferous forests at low to mid elevations, with a moss-dominated understory.

■ LOCAL SITES Very common; good concentrations on San Juan and Jedediah islands. Flowers July and August.

LADIES' TRESSES
Spiranthes romanzoffiana • Orchid family: *Orchidaceae*

■ DESCRIPTION This unusual orchid with its wonderful name, ladies' tresses, is a herbaceous perennial to 50 cm tall. Its lightly scented flowers are creamy-white, 1 cm long, and spiral around the stem in 3 vertical rows. The leaves are lanceolate, to 20 cm long and basal. The spiralling rows of flowers were thought to resemble a woman's braided hair.

78

■ HABITAT Diverse growing range; dry grassy fields and forests, bogs, streamsides and upper beaches.

■ LOCAL SITES Recorded on most of the islands; in short-grass areas at Ford Cove and Helliwell Provincial Park on Hornby Island; growing with rattlesnake plantain (*Goodyera oblongifolia*; see page 77) on roadsides on Galiano Island. Flowers July, August and September.

SPOTTED CORALROOT

Corallorhiza maculata ssp. *maculata* •
Orchid family: *Orchidaceae*

■ **DESCRIPTION** Spotted coralroot is a saprophyte to
60 cm in height. Its beautiful little flowers, to 1 cm long,
are reddish purple, with a white tongue marked with
crimson spots; they grow singularly along the stem. The
leaves are inconspicuous modified scales. The genus and
common names refer to the plant's coral-like roots.

■ **HABITAT** Moist shaded forests (usually conifer) at low
to mid elevations.

■ **LOCAL SITES**
Common; large patches
at Dionisio Point on
Galiano Island, trailside
from Mount Norman to
Beaumont Provincial
Marine Park on South
Pender Island and at
Ruckle Provincial Park
on Saltspring Island.
Flowers May and June.

FAIRYSLIPPER

Calypso bulbosa • Orchid family: *Orchidaceae*

■ DESCRIPTION Fairyslipper is a delicate herbaceous perennial from corm to 20 cm in height. Its flower is mauve to light purple; the lower lip is lighter and decorated with spots, stripes and coloured hairs. The single leaf is broadly lanceolate and withers with the flower; a new leaf appears in late summer and remains through winter. This is the most beautiful of the native orchids.

80

■ HABITAT Mostly associated with Douglas and grand fir forests.

■ NATIVE USE The Haida boiled and ate the corms in small quantities; they have a rich, buttery flavour.

■ LOCAL SITES Large concentrations on Jones, Sucia, Lopez, Orcas, Galiano, Portland and Wallace islands. Flowers April to May.

HEART-LEAFED TWAYBLADE
Listera cordata • Orchid family: *Orchidaceae*

■ DESCRIPTION Heart-leafed twayblade is a single-stemmed herbaceous perennial to 20 cm in height. Its flowers have a forked bottom lip and range from pale green to purplish. Twayblades have 2 heart-shaped opposite leaves that grow midway up the stem; *cordata* refers to these heart-shaped leaves.

■ HABITAT Most often associated with moist coniferous forests at low to mid elevations.

81

■ LOCAL SITES
On most of the Gulf and San Juan islands. Good selection at Beaumont Provincial Marine Park, on South Pender Island. Flowers May to June.

ELEGANT REIN-ORCHID
Piperia elegans • Orchid family: *Orchidaceae*

■ DESCRIPTION Elegant rein-orchid is a herbaceous perennial to 50 cm in height. Its tiny flowers are greenish white, with a protruding spur to 1 cm long: It's worth getting a close look at these beautiful, delicate flowers. Elegant rein-orchid has only 2 leaves, which wither by the time the flowers appear.

■ HABITAT Dry open coniferous forests at low elevations.

■ LOCAL SITES Good concentrations on San Juan and Gabriola islands. Flowers July to August.

82

BRITTLE PRICKLY-PEAR CACTUS
Opuntia fragilis • Cactus family: *Cactaceae*

■ DESCRIPTION Brittle prickly-pear cactus is a mat-forming, well-armed perennial to 60 cm across. Its yellow flowers are tissue-like, to 5 cm across. The leaves are modified to succulent stems, each carrying very pointed spines to 3 cm long.

■ HABITAT Dry exposed sites with well-drained soil.

■ NATIVE USE The sturdy, sharp spines were used to pierce ears.

■ LOCAL SITES Seen as far north as Helliwell Provincial Park on Hornby Island; lots in Jones Island State Marine Park and at Princess Bay on Portland Island. Flowers June and July.

HENDERSON'S SHOOTING STAR
Dodecatheon hendersonii • Primrose family: *Primulaceae*

■ DESCRIPTION Henderson's shooting star is a herbaceous perennial from 20-50 cm in height. Its attractive flowers are flaming pink, with 5 petals that sweep backwards. The leaves are basal and broadly ovate. The pointing anthers and windswept petals give this genus its name.

■ HABITAT Meadows and rocky knolls at low elevations.

■ LOCAL SITES Not common, making it a prize to find and just admire. Upland meadows on San Juan, Galiano and Saltspring islands. Flowers April to May.

KINNIKINNICK or BEARBERRY
Arctostaphylos uva-ursi • Heather family: *Ericaceae*

■**DESCRIPTION** Kinnikinnick is a trailing, mat-forming evergreen that rarely grows above 25 cm in height. Its fragrant, pinkish flowers bloom in spring and are replaced by bright red berries 1 cm across by late summer. The small, oval leaves grow to 3 cm long, are leathery and alternate. Grouse and bears feed on the berries.

■**HABITAT** Dry rocky outcrops and well-drained forest areas throughout B.C., from sea level to high elevations.

■**NATIVE USE**
Kinnikinnick is an eastern native word used to describe a tobacco mix. The leaves were dried and smoked, sometimes mixed with other plants.

■**LOCAL SITES** Cliffs above Ford Cove on Hornby Island, Drumbeg Provincial Park on Gabriola Island, and the surrounding small islands. Not as common on the San Juan Islands.

SALAL

Gaultheria shallon • Heather family: *Ericaceae*

■ **DESCRIPTION** Salal is a prostrate to mid-size bush that grows from 0.5 to 4 m in height. In spring the small pinkish flowers (1 cm long) hang like strings of tiny Chinese lanterns. The edible dark purple berries grow to 1 cm across and ripen by mid-August to September. Both the flowers and berries display themselves for several weeks. The dark green leaves are 7-10 cm long, tough and oval-shaped. Salal is often overlooked by berry pickers; the ripe berries taste excellent fresh and make fine preserves and wine.

■ **HABITAT** Dry to moist forested areas along the entire coast.

■ **NATIVE USE** Salal was an important food source for most native peoples. The berries were eaten fresh, mixed with other berries, or crushed and placed on skunk cabbage leaves to dry. The dried berry cakes were then rolled up and preserved for winter use.

■ **LOCAL SITES** Common understory bush and oceanside plant on most of the islands. Flowering starts beginning of May. Fruit starts to ripen beginning of August.

RED HUCKLEBERRY

Vaccinium parvifolium • Heather family: *Ericaceae*

■DESCRIPTION One of the most graceful of all B.C.'s berry bushes, the red huckleberry grows on old stumps, where it can attain heights of 3-4 m. The combination of almost translucent red berries (1 cm across), lacy zigzag branch structure and pale green leaves (oval, 2-5 cm long) is unmistakable. The small greenish to pink flowers are inconspicuous.

■HABITAT Coastal forested areas at lower elevations.

■NATIVE USE The berries were eaten fresh, mixed with other berries and dried for winter use. Their resemblance to salmon eggs made them ideal for fish bait.

■LOCAL SITES Good concentrations on Hornby, Denman, Ruxton, Galiano, Orcas and Sucia islands. Less common on the drier islands. Flowering starts mid-April and the berries ripen by the beginning of July.

EVERGREEN HUCKLEBERRY
Vaccinium ovatum • Heather family: *Ericaceae*

■DESCRIPTION Evergreen huckleberry is an attractive, mid-size shrub to 3 m in height. In spring it is covered in clusters of pinkish bell-shaped flowers. By late summer the branches are weighed down by the many small blue-black berries (5-7 mm across). This is a favourite late-season bush among avid berry pickers.

■HABITAT Coastal coniferous forests at low elevations.

■NATIVE USE The late-producing berries were in high demand for their flavour.

■LOCAL SITES Heavy concentrations in lower forested sites in Helliwell Provincial Park on Hornby Island and Campbell Point, on Mayne Island. Not common on the San Juan Islands, though recorded at Point Doughty on Orcas Island.

Mahonia nervosa • Barberry family: *Berberidaceae*

■**DESCRIPTION** Oregon grape is a smaller spreading understory shrub that is very noticeable when the bright yellow upright flowers are out. By midsummer the clusters of small green fruit (1 cm across) turn an attractive grape blue. The leaves are evergreen, holly-like, waxy and compound, with usually 9-17 leaflets. The bark is rough, light grey outside and brilliant yellow inside. Another species, tall Oregon grape (*M. aquifolium*), grows in a more open and dry location, is taller (2 m), and has fewer leaflets (5-9). The species name *aquifolium* means "holly-like."

■**HABITAT** Dry coniferous forests in southern coastal B.C. and Washington.

■**NATIVE USE** When steeped, the shredded stems of both species yield a yellow dye that was used in basket-making. The tart berries were usually mixed with sweeter berries for eating.

■**LOCAL SITES** Both species are a common understory plant, though tall Oregon grape is seen more on the southern Gulf Islands and on the San Juans. Flowering starts at the end of March. The berries begin to turn blue by mid-July and persist through autumn.

SASKATOON BERRY or SERVICEBERRY
Amelanchier alnifolia • Rose family: *Rosaceae*

■**DESCRIPTION** Depending on growing conditions, the saskatoon berry can vary from a 1-m shrub to a small tree 7 m in height. The white showy flowers range from 1 to 3 cm across and often hang in pendulous clusters. The young reddish berries form early and by midsummer darken to a purplish black up to 1 cm across. The light bluish green leaves are deciduous, oval-shaped and toothed above the middle.

■**HABITAT** Shorelines, rocky outcrops and open forests at low to mid elevations.

■**NATIVE USE** The berries were eaten fresh, mixed with other berries or dried for future use. On the great plains the berries were mashed with buffalo meat to make pemmican. The hard straight wood was a favourite for making arrows.

■**LOCAL SITES** Common; notably at Ford Cove on Hornby Island, Pirate's Cove on De Courcy Island, Herring Bay on Ruxton Island, Drumbeg Provincial Park on Gabriola Island, Moran State Park on Orcas Island. Flowering starts mid-April and the berries are fully ripe by the first week of August.

THIMBLEBERRY

Rubus parviflorus • Rose family: *Rosaceae*

■DESCRIPTION Thimbleberry is an unarmed shrub to 3 m in height. Its large white flowers open up to 5 cm across and are replaced by juicy bright red berries. The dome-shaped berries are 2 cm across and bear little resemblance to a thimble. The maple-shaped leaves grow up to 25 cm across and, when needed, make a good tissue substitute.

■HABITAT Common in coastal B.C. and Washington in open forests at low to mid elevations.

■NATIVE USE The large leaves were used to line cooking pits and cover baskets. The berries were eaten fresh, dried or mixed with other berries.

■LOCAL SITES Common in moist forest sites on the larger islands, particularly Ruxton, Gabriola, Hornby, Orcas and San Juan. Flowering starts mid-May and the fruit matures at the end of July or in early August.

BLACKBERRIES
Rubus sps • *Rose family* • Rosaceae

■DESCRIPTION Of B.C.'s three blackberry species, only one is native to the region. The two introduced species require more sunshine to thrive. The three are easy to identify:
Trailing blackberry (*Rubus ursinus*) — the first to bloom (end of April) and set fruit (mid-July), it is often seen rambling over plants in and out of forested areas. The berries are delicious and the leaves can be steeped as a tea.
Himalayan blackberry (*R. discolor*) — this blackberry was introduced from India and has now taken over much of the Pacific Northwest. It is heavily armed, grows rampant to 10 m and is a prolific producer of berries. Blooming starts mid-June and the fruit sets by mid-August.
Cutleaf blackberry (*R. laciniatus*) — introduced from Europe, this berry is very similar to the Himalayan blackberry but less common.
■HABITAT Common on open wasteland, forest edges, roadsides and in ditches.
■LOCAL SITES Trailing blackberry is very common on most of the Gulf Islands. All 3 species can be seen on the larger inhabited islands.

Cutleaf blackberry

Himalayan blackberry

Trailing blackberry

< *Ripe trailing blackberries*

SALMONBERRY

Rubus spectabilis • Rose family: *Rosaceae*

■DESCRIPTION Salmonberry is one of B.C.'s tallest native berry bushes. Though it averages 2-3 m, the bush can grow up to 4 m high. The pink bell-shaped flowers, 3-4 cm across, bloom at the end of February and are a welcome sight. Flowering continues until June, when both the flowers and ripe fruit can be seen on the same bush. The soft logan-shaped berries range in colour from yellow to orange to red, with the occasional dark purple. The leaves are compound, with 3 leaflets, much like the leaves of a raspberry. Weak prickles may be seen on the lower portion of the branches; the tops are unarmed. The berry's common name comes from its resemblance to the shape and colour of salmon eggs.

■HABITAT Common on the coast of B.C. and Washington in shaded damp forests.

■NATIVE USE The high water content in the berries prevented them from being stored for any length of time. They were generally eaten shortly after harvesting.

■LOCAL SITES Forms thickets in moist forested valleys on the larger islands. Flowering starts in March, with the fruit ripening at the end of May to July.

BLACK RASPBERRY or BLACKCAP
Rubus leucodermis • Rose family: *Rosaceae*

■DESCRIPTION Black raspberry is a deciduous armed shrub to 2 m in height. Its white flowers are small, to 3 cm across and borne in terminal clusters of 3-7. The resulting fruit (1 cm across) starts off red but turns dark purple to black by July and August. The leaves have 3-5 leaflets supported on long, arching, well-armed stems. Black raspberries can be distinguished from other raspberries by the bloom, a whitish waxy coating, on the stems.

■HABITAT Open forests and edges at low to mid elevations.

■NATIVE USE The berries were eaten raw or dried into cakes for winter consumption.

■LOCAL SITES Common on most of the islands, particularly San Juan, Lopez, Saturna and Saltspring.

WOODLAND STRAWBERRY
Fragaria vesca • Rose family: *Rosaceae*

■DESCRIPTION Woodland strawberry is an unarmed herbaceous perennial to 20 cm in height. Its white flowers, 1-3 cm across, have 5 petals and a yellow centre. The delicious fruit, 1-3 cm across, is a small version of the cultivated strawberry. The leaves are compound, 3-5 cm across, and have 3 coarsely toothed leaflets. The blue-leaf or wild strawberry (*F. virginiana*) is similar to the woodland strawberry with two differences: the blue-leaf has bluish green leaves and the terminal teeth on its leaflets are shorter than the teeth on either side; the terminal teeth of the woodland strawberry are longer than the others.

■HABITAT Mainly in lower open forests, but can be found at mid to high elevations.

■NATIVE USE The juicy fruit was eaten fresh, the leaves were steeped for tea.

■LOCAL SITES Common on the islands; large patches on Mount Norman on South Pender Island and at Dionisio Point, Coon Bay and Maple Bay on Galiano Island. Flowers May and June.

BLACK GOOSEBERRY or BLACK SWAMP GOOSEBERRY
Ribes lacustre •
Currant and Gooseberry family: *Grossulariaceae*

■**DESCRIPTION** Black gooseberry is an armed shrub to 2 m in height. Its delicate reddish flowers are disc-shaped, to 0.5 cm across, and hang in drooping clusters of 7-15. The small, dark purple berries are bristly and hang in clusters of 3-4. The leaves are maple-shaped, with 5 lobes, from 2-5 cm across. The branches are covered with small golden spines, with larger spines at the nodes. Use caution when picking the berries: the spines can cause an allergic reaction in some people.

■**HABITAT** Moist open forests, lake edges at low to high elevations.

■**NATIVE USE** The berries were eaten by most groups.

■**LOCAL SITES** A common berry bush on the San Juan Islands; less common on the Gulf Islands. Berries ripen July to August.

SOOPOLALLIE, SOAPBERRY or CANADIAN BUFFALO BERRY
Shepherdia canadensis • Oleaster family: *Elaeagnaceae*

■DESCRIPTION Soopolallie is a deciduous bush 1-3 m in height. The tiny bronze, star-like male and female flowers are borne on separate bushes. The bitter berries are bright red and grow in small clusters along the stems. The leaves and stems are covered with orange dots, giving them a rusty appearance. Soopolallie is Chinook for "soapberry," referring to the way the berries froth up when beaten with water.
■HABITAT Forest edges, upper beaches, at low to mid elevations.

98

■NATIVE USE Ice cream was made from the froth of the berries.
■LOCAL SITES Common; good concentrations on Lopez, Shaw, Galiano and Saltspring islands. Flowers end of March to April. Berries ripen by mid-July.

Athyrium filix-femina • Polypody family: *Polypodiaceae*

■DESCRIPTION Lady fern is a tall fragile fern to 2 m in
height. The apple green fronds average up to 30 cm across
and are widest below the centre, tapering at top and bottom.
This diamond shape distinguishes the lady fern from the
similar-looking spiny wood fern (*Dryopteris expansa*) whose
fronds have an abrupt triangular form. The fronds die off in
winter and emerge again in April. The horseshoe-shaped sori
appear on the back of the fronds in spring.

■HABITAT Moist forests with nutrient-rich soils.
■NATIVE USE The young fronds (fiddleheads) were
sometimes eaten in April.
■LOCAL SITES Common; wonderful groves on lower damp
trails in Beaumont Provincial Marine Park on South Pender
Island; also on Jedediah, Hornby and Denman islands.

MAIDENHAIR FERN

Adiantum pedatum • Polypody family: *Polypodiaceae*

■**DESCRIPTION** Maidenhair fern is a delicate-looking fern with an almost tropical appearance. The fan-shaped fronds carry the dainty green leaflets (pinnules), which contrast well with the dark stems (stipes) that grow up to 60 cm in length. The reproducing sori under the pinnules are visible in late summer and fall. The genus name *Adiantum*, meaning "unwetted," refers to the way the fronds repel water.

■**HABITAT** Moist cliff faces at low to mid elevations.

■**NATIVE USE**
The shiny black stipes were used in basket-making.

■**LOCAL SITES** Reported by waterfalls above Cascade Lake and stream banks near Mount Constitution on Orcas Island; also on Saturna, Mayne, Galiano, Pender and Saltspring islands.

DEER FERN

Blechnum spicant • Polypody family: *Polypodiaceae*

■DESCRIPTION Deer fern can be distinguished from licorice fern (*Polypodium glycyrrhiza*; see page 106) and sword fern (*Polystichum munitum*; see page 105) by its two distinct types of frond, sterile and fertile. The sterile fronds grow up to 75 cm long, are tapered at both ends and usually lie flat. The fertile or spore-producing fronds are erect from the centre of the plant and can grow up to 75 cm in height. Deer ferns are good winter browse for deer.

■HABITAT Moist forested areas with plenty of rainfall.

■LOCAL SITES More common on the northern islands; reported on Blakely and Orcas islands; huge groves on Jedediah Island, in association with western sword fern (*Polystichum munitum*) under a canopy of bigleaf maple (*Acer macrophyllum*; see page 147) and grand fir (*Abies grandis*; see page 169).

SPINY WOOD FERN or SHIELD FERN
Dryopteris expansa • Polypody family: *Polypodiaceae*

■DESCRIPTION Spiny wood fern is an elegant plant to
1.5 m tall. The pale green fronds are triangular in shape,
average up to 25 cm across and die off in winter. In spring
the rounded sori are produced on the underside of the fronds.
Spiny wood fern is similar in appearance and requirements
to lady fern (*Athryium filix-femina*; see page 99).
■HABITAT Common in moist forests at low to mid
elevations.

■LOCAL SITES Common in dense moist forests, usually
seen on rotting stumps.

BRACKEN FERN

Pteridium aquilinum • Polypody family: *Polypodiaceae*

■**DESCRIPTION** Bracken fern is B.C.'s tallest native fern, often reaching 3 m or more in height. It is also the most widespread fern in the world. The tall, arching fronds are dark green with a golden green stem (stipe), triangular in shape, and grow singly from rhizomes in spring.

■**HABITAT** Has a diverse growing range, from dry to moist and open to forested regions.

■**NATIVE USE** The rhizomes were peeled and eaten fresh or cooked, and the fiddleheads were boiled and eaten. However, it is not advisable to eat this fern as it has now been proven to be a health hazard.

■**LOCAL SITES** Bracken fern has found its place on all the Gulf Islands, even on Isle de Lis.

WESTERN SWORD FERN
Polystichum munitum • Polypody family: *Polypodiaceae*

■DESCRIPTION Western sword fern is southern B.C.'s most common fern. It is evergreen and can grow to 1.5 m in height. The fronds are dark green with side leaves (pinnae) that are sharply pointed and toothed. On the underside of the fronds a double row of sori forms midsummer and turns orange by autumn. The fronds are in high demand in eastern Canada for floral decorations. The species name *munitum* means "armed," referring to the side leaves that resemble swords.

■HABITAT Dry to moist forest at lower elevations near the coast, where it can form pure groves.

■NATIVE USE The ferns were used to line steaming pits and baskets, and were placed on floors as sleeping mats.

■LOCAL SITES Common; extensive understory groves on Jedediah Island and between Devina Drive and Maple Bay on Galiano Island.

105

LICORICE FERN

Polypodium glycyrrhiza • Polypody family: *Polypodiaceae*

■DESCRIPTION Licorice fern is a smaller evergreen fern commonly seen on mossy slopes and on the trunks of bigleaf maple trees. The dark green fronds grow to 50 cm long and 5-7 cm wide and have a golden stem (stipe). The round spores are produced in a single row under the leaves. The rhizomes have a licorice taste, hence the fern's common name.

106

■HABITAT Low-elevation forests, where it grows on trunks and branches of large trees, sometimes on shady outcrops.

■NATIVE USE The roots were eaten fresh or cooked and were also used as a cold and throat medicine.

■LOCAL SITES Abundant on the more northern islands, less common on the San Juans.

MANROOT or BIGROOT

Marah oreganus • Cucumber family: *Cucurbitaceae*

■DESCRIPTION Manroot is a climbing herbaceous perennial to lengths of over 7 m. It has separate female and male flowers that grow on the same plant: The white bell-shaped female flowers to 1 cm across are formed singly, and the males grow in small clusters. The fleshy fruit, to 8 cm across, resembles miniature bristly rugby balls; in August the bottoms of the fruit burst open to reveal the large seeds (2 cm long). The palmate leaves alternate from the stalk and grow 10-20 cm across.

■HABITAT Open fields, hillsides and forest edges at low elevations.

■NATIVE USE A mixture was made from the plant to treat venereal disease.

■LOCAL SITES This unusual plant can be seen growing on the open hillsides going up Mount Constitution on Orcas Island. Common on the San Juan Islands.

ROUND-LEAFED SUNDEW
Drosera rotundifolia • Sundew family: *Droseraceae*

■DESCRIPTION There are about 100 species of sundew around the world, and all of them eat insects. B.C. and Washington's native round-leafed sundew is a small perennial, 5-25 cm high, with inconspicuous white flowers. It is the leaves that make this plant a curiosity. They are equipped with fine red hairs, each tipped with a shiny globe of reddish secretion. Small insects are attracted to the secretion and get stuck in it; the leaf then slowly folds over and smothers the unsuspecting visitors. The plant's favourite foods are mosquitoes, gnats and midges.

■HABITAT Peat bogs throughout the west coast of B.C.

■NATIVE USE The whole plant is acrid, and the leaves were once used to remove corns, warts and bunions.

■LOCAL SITES Summit Lake on Orcas Island; Beaverton Marsh on San Juan Island; Blakely and Galiano islands.

Typha latifolia • Cat-tail family: *Typhaceae*

■DESCRIPTION Cat-tails are semi-aquatic perennials that can grow to 2.5 m in height. The distinctive "tail," a brown spike, is 15-20 cm long and 3 cm wide and made up of male and female flowers. The lighter-coloured male flowers grow at the top and usually fall off, leaving a bare spike above the familiar brown female flowers. The sword-shaped leaves are alternate and spongy at the base.

■HABITAT Common in B.C. at low to mid elevations, at lakesides and riversides and in ponds, marshes and ditches.

109

■NATIVE USE The long leaves were used to weave mats and the fluffy seeds to stuff pillows and mattresses.

■LOCAL SITES Common on most of the Gulf Islands. Large concentrations at Smuggler's Lake Park on Protection Island.

RUNNING CLUBMOSS
Lycopodium clavatum • Clubmoss family: *Lycopodiaceae*

■DESCRIPTION Running clubmoss is a curious creeping evergreen that looks like it is made of bright green pipe cleaners. Like all clubmosses, it has no flowers and reproduces by spores. These are held in terminal cones on vertical stalks to 25 cm in height. The evergreen leaves are lance-shaped and arranged spirally around the stem. Running clubmoss grows horizontally across the ground, with irregular rooting. The spores are used medicinally and in industry.

■HABITAT Dry to moist coniferous forests at low to high elevations.

■LOCAL SITES Not common; found on Mountain Lake and Twin Lakes trail on Orcas Island, Mount Gibraltar on Jedediah Island and on Blakely, Saturna, Galiano and South Pender islands.

STINGING NETTLE
Urtica dioica • Nettle family: *Urticaceae*

■DESCRIPTION Stinging nettle is a herbaceous perennial to over 2 m in height. Its tiny flowers are greenish and produced in hanging clusters to 5 cm long. The leaves are heart-shaped at the base, tapered to the top, coarsely toothed, to 10 cm long. The stalks, stems and leaves all have stinging hairs that contain formic acid; many people have the misfortune of encountering this plant the hard way. The genus name *Urtica* is from the Latin *uro* ("to burn").

■HABITAT Thrives in moist, nutrient-rich, somewhat shady disturbed sites, where it can form great masses. Stinging nettles are usually an indicator of nitrogen-rich soil.

■NATIVE USE The young leaves were boiled as a spinach substitute.

■LOCAL SITES Common on most of the islands; forms dense roadside thickets on Galiano Island.

SEABEACH SANDWORT
Honkenya peploides • Pink family: *Caryophyllaceae*

■DESCRIPTION Seabeach sandwort is a herbaceous perennial to 30 cm in height. Its odd-looking flowers are greenish white, to 1.5 cm across and held in terminal leaf whorls. The fleshy leaves are elliptic, pale green, opposite, to 5 cm long. Sandwort can be seen growing as a single plant or as a mat to 1 m across. The genus name is after G. Honckeny, an 18th-century German botanist.

■HABITAT Upper sandy beaches, between rocks and logs.

■LOCAL SITES Most common on Lopez Island in the San Juan Islands and at Norman Point on Hornby Island.

112

SCOURING RUSH
Equisetum hyemale • Horsetail family: *Equisetaceae*

■DESCRIPTION Scouring rush is a herbaceous perennial to 1.7 m in height. Its dark green stems are all alike, with black rings separating the hollow sections. They are branchless and rough or scratchy to touch. Like ferns, horsetails do not produce flowers or fruit but reproduce from spores. These are borne in hard, pointed terminal cones.

■HABITAT Usually close to fresh water, by streams and rivers or at the base of moist slopes with loose rich soil.

113

■NATIVE USE The abrasive stems were used as sandpaper and the dark roots to make baskets.

■LOCAL SITES Common on most of the Gulf Islands; good concentrations at Montague Harbour on Galiano Island; extensive patches at lower sites around Tribune Bay on Hornby Island.

COMMON HORSETAIL
Equisetum arvense • Horsetail family: *Equisetaceae*

■DESCRIPTION Common horsetail is a herbaceous perennial to 75 cm in height. It has two types of stems, fertile and sterile, both hollow except at the nodes. The fertile stems are unbranched, to 30 cm in height, and lack chlorophyll; they bear spores in the terminal head. The green sterile stems grow to 75 cm in height and have leaves whorled at the joints. Horsetails are all that is left of a prehistoric family, some members of which grew to the size of trees.

115

■HABITAT Low wet seepage areas, meadows, damp sandy soils and gravel roads from low to high elevations.

■LOCAL SITES Common on most of the Gulf Islands. Wonderful groupings between Maple Bay and Dionisio Point on Galiano Island.

BULL KELP
Nereocystis luetkeana • Brown algae family: *Phaeophyceae*

■DESCRIPTION Bull kelp is B.C.'s largest marine alga, to 30 m in length. It is held on the ocean floor by root-like holdfasts. At this point the stalk is very thin, but it increases in diameter until it terminates in a bulbous float to 15 cm wide. Attached to the float are clusters of brownish leaf-like blades to 4.5 m long.

■HABITAT Ocean outside the low tide zone, usually in at least 6 m of water with a rocky bottom. In protected areas it can form several hectares of beds.

■NATIVE USE The floats were used as containers to hold eulachon grease, fish oil and, more recently, molasses. The thin stalks were made into fishing lines, nets and rope.

■LOCAL SITES Common; large beds off Drumbeg Provincial Park on Gabriola Island.

SILVER BURWEED

Ambrosia chamissonis • Aster family: *Asteraceae*

■DESCRIPTION Silver burweed is a coastal herbaceous perennial to 1 m in height/length. Its flowers are separate, with males in terminal heads and females in the lower leaf axils. The felty leaves are deeply divided, silvery green, to 7 cm long.

■HABITAT Coastal sandy beaches, between logs and rocks.

■LOCAL SITES Common beach plant on the islands; large patches at Downes Point and Grassy Point on Hornby Island. Flowers June to August.

117

AMERICAN SEAROCKET
Cakile edentula • Mustard family: *Brassicaceae*

■**DESCRIPTION** American searocket is a coastal sprawling annual to 50 cm in height / length. Its pink to mauve flowers form towards the end of the stems and are up to 8 cm long. The odd-looking leaves are oblong, to 7 cm long and, like the stems, fleshy. When ripe, the pod-like fruit break up easily in the waves.

■**HABITAT** Coastal sandy beaches, prefers long shallow tides.

■**LOCAL SITES** San Juan, Lopez, Saturna and Cabbage islands; huge displays on sandy beaches between Norman Point and Downes Point on Hornby Island. Flowers mid-June to July.

SEA ASPARAGUS or AMERICAN GLASSWORT
Salicornia virginica • Goosefoot family: *Chenopodiaceae*

■DESCRIPTION Sea asparagus is an edible perennial to 30 cm in height. Its tiny yellow-green flowers grow in threes in small sunken cavities along the succulent stems. The scale-like leaves are almost non-existent. As its name suggests, the young stems of this wild green vegetable can be collected and eaten raw or cooked. They have a salty flavour, but it can be masked with a few herbs.

■HABITAT Common along the B.C. and Washington coastline in areas with little wave action. Can form dense colonies to hundreds of square metres in tidal flats and salt marshes.

■LOCAL SITES Common; large colonies at Montague Harbour on Gabriola Island, Fisherman Bay on Lopez Island, Argyle Lagoon on San Juan Island and Downes Point on Hornby Island. Flowers July to August.

ROCKWEED or POPPING WRACK
Fucus sp. • Brown alga family: *Phaeophyceae*

■DESCRIPTION Rockweed is an intertidal seaweed (alga) from 15 to 60 cm in length. Its branches are flat, brown, leathery and thick through the middle, with inflated ends. It attaches itself to intertidal rocks with a small, disc-like holdfast.

■HABITAT Rocky beaches along the coastline.

■NATIVE USE Children used to step on the swollen ends to make them pop — hence the common name "popping wrack." On hot days, fishermen placed rockweed over their catch to keep it cool.

■LOCAL SITES Common on rocky beaches. Campbell Point on Mayne Island has a good collection.

SEA PLANTAIN

Plantago maritima ssp. *juncoides* •
Plantain family: *Plantaginaceae*

DESCRIPTION Sea plantain is a coastal beach perennial
to 30 cm in height. Its flowers are typical of plantain —
small, greenish and tightly grouped on stiff spikes to
30 cm. The leaves are pale green, fleshy, basal, erect and
slightly shorter than the flower spikes. Its sharp leaves
and flower spikes make this plant easy to recognize.

HABITAT Sandy ocean shorelines and saline marshes.

LOCAL SITES Common on the islands.

PLANTAIN

Plantago spp. • Plantain family: *Plantaginaceae*

■**DESCRIPTION** Ribwort plantain (*P. lanceolata*; below, left) and common plantain (*P. major*; below, right) are introduced perennials that have made weeds of themselves worldwide. Ribwort grows to 60 cm in height, has curious flowers and long, basal, lance-shaped leaves. Common plantain grows to 40 cm in height and has tight spikes of green flowers and large oval leaves.

■**HABITAT** Both species invade lawns and roadsides at low to mid elevations.

■**LOCAL SITES** Common; ribwort has taken a strong foothold on Discovery Island.

CANDY STICK or BARBER POLE
Allotropa virgata • Indian pipe family: *Monotropaceae*

■DESCRIPTION Appropriately named, candy stick is a red-and-white-striped saphrophyte 15-60 cm in height. Its flowers have white to pink sepals, a central red ovary with 10 very noticeable red stamens. The leaves are reduced to small, lance-shaped scales. The species name *virgata* is Latin for "striped."

■HABITAT Moist coniferous forests at low to mid elevations.

123

■LOCAL SITES Not common; a treasure to find. Recorded on Saturna and Galiano islands. Flowers June to July.

YELLOW POND LILY
Nuphar polysepalum • Water lily family: *Nymphaeaceae*

■ **DESCRIPTION** Yellow pond lily is a long-stemmed aquatic perennial. Its striking yellow flowers to 10 cm across are a familiar summer sight in lakes and ponds. A large round stigma dominates the centre of these large, waxy flowers. The heart-shaped floating leaves, or pads, grow to 40 cm long. The huge rhizomes when exposed at low water levels are sought after by bears. The genus name *Nuphar* means water lily.

■ **HABITAT** Ponds, lakes, marshes at low to mid elevations.

■ **NATIVE USE** The seeds, called *wok as*, were gathered and used as a food source.

■ **LOCAL SITES** Common; good concentrations in small lakes and ponds in Moran State Park on Orcas Island. Flowering begins in May and continues through the summer.

INDIAN PIPE
Monotropa uniflora • Indian Pipe family: *Monotropaceae*

■**DESCRIPTION** Indian Pipe is a fleshy ghost-like herbaceous perennial to 25 cm in height. It has a single white flower (hence the species name, *uniflora*), to 3 cm long; this starts off nodding but stands erect when mature. The leaves are white, scale-like and clasp the stem. The entire plant turns black at the end of the growing season. The plant is usually seen growing in clumps of up to 25 stems.

■**HABITAT** Coniferous forests with nutrient-rich soil and deep shade at low elevations.

■**LOCAL SITES** Common on the densely forested islands, especially on Portland Island, in Beaumont Provincial Marine Park on South Pender Island, Montague Harbour on Galiano Island, Ford Cove on Hornby Island. Flowers early July.

NAKED BROOMRAPE or
ONE-FLOWERED CANCER-ROOT
Orobanche uniflora • Broomrape family: *Orobanchaceae*

■**DESCRIPTION** Naked broomrape is a parasitic annual to 15 cm in height. Its single flower is purple with a whitish throat, to 2 cm long; there are usually 1 to 3 flower stalks on each plant. Naked broomrape receives its nourishment from the roots of other plants.

■**HABITAT** Rock outcrops, open slopes, and wherever broad-leafed stonecrops grow.

■**LOCAL SITES** Common; lots on Orcas, Portland and Saltspring islands. Flowers mid-April to July.

127

OCEANSPRAY
Holodiscus discolor • Rose family: *Rosaceae*

■DESCRIPTION Oceanspray is an upright, deciduous shrub to 5 m in height. Its small, creamy-white flowers are densely packed to form reversed pyramidal clusters to 20 cm long. The fruiting clusters turn an unattractive brown and persist through winter. The leaves are wedge-shaped, flat green above, pale green and hairy below, to 5 cm long. The species name *discolor* refers to the two-coloured leaf.

■HABITAT Dry open forests at low to mid elevations; often found on rocky outcrops.

■NATIVE USE The straight new growth was a favourite for making arrows, hence its other name, arrow-wood. The wood is extremely hard and was used to make harpoon shafts, teepee pins, digging tools and drum hoops.

■LOCAL SITES Common; good concentrations can be seen on Jedediah Island, at Pirate's Cove on De Courcy Island and along the coastline of San Juan and Jones islands. In full flower by the end of June.

NOOTKA ROSE
Rosa nutkana • Rose family: *Rosaceae*

■DESCRIPTION The largest of B.C.'s native roses, the Nootka rose grows to 3 m in height. The showy pink flowers are 5-petalled, fragrant, 5 cm across and usually solitary. The compound leaves have 5-7 toothed leaflets and are armed with a pair of prickles underneath. The reddish hips are round and plump, 1-2 cm across, and contrast well with the dark green foliage.

■HABITAT Open low-elevation forests throughout B.C.

■NATIVE USE Rosehips were strung together to make necklaces and the flowers were pressed to make perfume. Rosehips were eaten only in times of famine.

■LOCAL SITES One of the most common bushes on the Gulf Islands; extensive thickets roadside and seaside on Galiano Island. Flowers mid-May and the hips start to develop colour in August.

BALDHIP or WOODLAND ROSE
Rosa gymnocarpa • Rose family: *Rosaceae*

■DESCRIPTION The baldhip rose is B.C.'s and Washington's smallest native rose. It is often prostrate, to 1.4 m in height. The tiny pink flowers are 5-petalled, delicately fragrant, 1-2 cm across and usually solitary. The compound leaves are smaller than the Nootka rose and have 5-9 toothed leaflets. The spindly stems are mostly armed with weak prickles. A good identifier is this rose's unusual habit of losing its sepals, leaving the hip bald — hence the species name *gymnocarpa*, which means "naked fruit." Rosehips have a higher concentration of vitamin C than oranges and make an excellent jelly or marmalade.

■HABITAT Dry open forests at lower elevations, from southern B.C. to the redwood forests of California.

■LOCAL SITES Not as common as the Nootka rose (*R. Nutkana*); more dominant on the San Juan Islands, with good representation on Orcas, Crane and Jones islands. Flowers end of May.

HARDHACK or STEEPLEBUSH
Spiraea douglasii • Rose family: *Rosaceae*

■DESCRIPTION Hardhack is an upright deciduous bush to 2 m in height. Its tiny pink flowers group together to form fuzzy pyramidal clusters up to 15 cm tall. The resulting brown fruiting clusters persist on the bush through winter. The alternate leaves are elliptic to oval, toothed above the middle, 5-10 cm long, dark green above and a felty paler green below.

■HABITAT Prefers moist conditions, can be seen growing in ditches and bogs and at lakesides from low levels to subalpine meadows.

■NATIVE USE The tough wiry branches were used to make halibut hooks, scrapers and hooks for drying and smoking salmon.

■LOCAL SITES Thickets roadside on Saltspring Island; low areas around Tribune Bay on Hornby Island and on central Portland Island. Flowering begins mid-June and fades by August.

INDIAN PLUM
Oemleria cerasiformis • Rose family: *Rosaceae*

■DESCRIPTION Indian plum is an upright deciduous shrub or small tree to 5 m in height. Its flowers, which usually emerge before the leaves, are white, 1 cm across, and hang in clusters 6-10 cm long. The small, plum-like fruit grow to 1 cm across; they start off yellowish red and finish a bluish black. They are edible, but a large seed and bitter taste make them better left for the birds. The leaves are broadly lance-shaped, light green, 7-12 cm long, and appear in upright clusters. The species name *cerasiformis* means "cherry-shaped," a reference to the fruit.

■HABITAT Restricted to low elevations on the southern coast and Gulf Islands; prefers moist, open broad-leafed forests.

■NATIVE USE Small amounts were eaten fresh or dried for winter use.

■LOCAL SITES Rare in the San Juan Islands, though recorded at Eagle Cove and Cady Mountain on San Juan Island. More common on the northern Gulf Islands including Gabriola, Newcastle and Hornby. Flowers March to April, with ripe fruit by the end of June.

NINEBARK

Physocarpus capitatus • Rose family: *Rosaceae*

DESCRIPTION Ninebark is an upright deciduous shrub to 4 m in height. Its tiny white flowers are grouped into rounded clusters to 7 cm across. The fruit are reddish brown, inflated seed capsules. The maple-shaped leaves are 3- to 5- lobed, shiny green above, paler below, to 7 cm long. It is debatable whether the shaggy bark has nine layers. The species name *capitatus* refers to the rounded heads of the flowers.

HABITAT Usually seen on moist sites, in open forests and at streams and lakesides, but also on dry rocky areas at lower elevations.

NATIVE USE Ninebark was used medicinally.

LOCAL SITES Rare on the San Juan Islands; lots on Hornby and Denman islands, Herring Bay on Ruxton Island and between Sylva Bay and Drumbeg Provincial Park on Gabriola Island. Flowers June; seed heads persist through autumn.

RED-BERRIED ELDER or RED ELDERBERRY
Sambucus racemosa • Honeysuckle family: *Caprifoliaceae*

■DESCRIPTION Red-berried elder is a bushy shrub to 6 m in height. Its small flowers are creamy-white and grow in pyramidal clusters 10-20 cm long. The berries that replace them take up to 3 months to turn bright red; they are considered poisonous to people when eaten raw but are a favourite food for birds. The leaves are compound, 5-15 cm long, with 5-9 opposite leaflets.

CAUTION: the berries are considered poisonous.

135

■HABITAT Moist coastal forest edges and roadsides. The blue-berried elder (*S. caerulea*) is found more in the Interior and the Gulf Islands.

■NATIVE USE The pithy branches were hollowed out and used as blowguns.

■LOCAL SITES Common on the islands that have damp forests; large specimens seen on De Courcy Island. Flowering starts mid-April, berries turn bright red late June.

BLUE-BERRIED ELDER or BLUE ELDERBERRY
Sambucus caerulea • Honeysuckle family: *Caprifoliaceae*

■DESCRIPTION Blue-berried elder ranges from a bush to a small tree that grows to 6 m in height. Its flowers are similar to those of the red-berried elder but are in flat-topped clusters, not pyramidal. The mature berries are dark blue with a white coating of bloom, giving them a soft blue appearance. The leaves are compound, with 5 to 9 oval, lance-shaped leaflets.

■HABITAT Dry open sites at low elevations.

■NATIVE USE Though the raw berries are edible, they were usually eaten cooked.

■LOCAL SITES Large 6 m specimens at Shingle Spit ferry terminal on Hornby Island, roadsides on Gabriola Island and along the west side of San Juan Island. The berries start to turn blue by mid-August and, if not eaten by birds or people, last into October.

SNOWBERRY

Symphoricarpos albus • Honeysuckle family: *Caprifoliaceae*

■**DESCRIPTION** Snowberry is an erect deciduous shrub to 2 m in height. Its small white to pink flowers turn into an abundance of very noticeable white berries 1-2 cm across. Older plants produce a smaller oval leaf to 2 cm long, while younger, more vigorous plants have wavy leaves to 5 cm long. The leaves have a sweet fragrance when wet. Snowberries are best appreciated in winter, when the bright white berries stand out against the surrounding grey. The genus name *Symphoricarpos* refers to the clustering of the berries.

CAUTION: the berries are considered poisonous.

■**HABITAT** Open forested areas at low to mid elevations.

■**NATIVE USE** Thin branches were hollowed out to make pipe stems and larger branches were bound together to make brooms.

■**LOCAL SITES** A very common shrub; dense thickets on Gabriola and Jones islands. Flowers mid-June to July. White berries noticeable by September.

BLACK TWINBERRY

Lonicera involucrata • Honeysuckle family: *Caprifoliaceae*

■DESCRIPTION Black twinberry is a deciduous shrub 1-3 m in height. Its yellow flowers are tubular and borne in pairs, to 2 cm long. The inedible berries are shiny black, cupped in a moon bract, to 1 cm across. The leaves are broadly lance-shaped, tapering to a point, opposite, 5-15 cm long.

■HABITAT Moist to wet open forests at low to high elevations.

■NATIVE USE The berries were mashed and the purple juice used to dye roots for basketry. The Haida rubbed the berries into their scalps to prevent their hair from turning grey. It was said that eating the berries drove a person crazy.

■LOCAL SITES Rare on the southern Gulf Islands, reported as fairly common in damp areas on the San Juan Islands. Good concentrations at Tribune Bay on Hornby Island. Flowering starts mid-May, with the berries appearing mid-June.

WESTERN BOG LAUREL

Kalmia microphylla ssp. *occidentalis* • Heather family: *Ericaceae*

■DESCRIPTION B.C.'s and Washington's native laurel is a small lanky evergreen no more than 60 cm high. Its beautiful pink flowers (2.5 cm across) have a built-in pollen dispenser. A close look reveals that some of the stamens are bent over; these spring up when the flower is disturbed, dusting the intruder with pollen. The leaves are opposite, lance-shaped, 2-4 cm long, shiny dark green above, felty white below, with edges strongly rolled over. The plant is poisonous and should

not be confused with Labrador tea (*Ledum groenlandicum*; see page 140), which it resembles from above.

CAUTION: the plant is poisonous.

■HABITAT Peat bogs and lakeshores at low to high elevations throughout B.C. and Washington.

■NATIVE USE The leaves were boiled and used in small doses for medicinal purposes.

■LOCAL SITES In early May this is a fabulous plant to find in full flower. Recorded at Summit Lake on Orcas Island, Beaverton Marsh on San Juan Island and on Galiano and Saltspring islands.

LABRADOR TEA

Ledum groenlandicum • Heather family: *Ericaceae*

■DESCRIPTION Most of the year, Labrador tea is a gangly small shrub to 1.4 m in height. In spring the masses of small white flowers turn it into the Cinderella of the bog. The evergreen leaves are lance-shaped, alternate, 4-6 cm long, with the edges rolled over. The leaves can be distinguished from those of the poisonous bog laurel (*Kalmia microphylla*; see page 139) by their flat green colour on top and rusty-coloured hairs beneath. To be safe, only pick the leaves when the shrub is in flower.

■HABITAT Peat bogs, lakesides and permanent wet meadows, low to alpine elevations.

■NATIVE USE The leaves have long been used by native groups across Canada and the U.S. as infusions. Early explorers and settlers quickly picked up on this caffeine substitute. Caution must be taken — not all people can drink it.

■LOCAL SITES Sphagnum bogs at Summit Lake, on Orcas Island and on Mayne and Galiano islands. Flowers mid-May to June.

SCOTCH BROOM

Cytisus scoparius • Pea family: *Leguminosae*

■**DESCRIPTION** Scotch broom is a mid-size, unarmed, deciduous shrub to 3 m in height. The bright yellow, pea-like flowers are 2 cm long and project at all angles from the stems. When the flowering period is over, the bushes are draped with thousands of brown-black pods up to 5 cm long. These pods split open when dry, forcing the seeds several metres away from the parent plant. The leaves are short and narrow and pressed close to the stems. A native of Scotland, broom was introduced near Victoria in the mid-1800s and has since become an invasive weed on southern Vancouver Island and the adjoining coast. As its common name suggests, its branches were tied together and used as a broom.

■**HABITAT** Dry sites, rocky outcrops, roadsides and parkland.

■**LOCAL SITES** Scotch broom has become a serious invader on the islands; as beautiful as it looks in flower, it is crowding out the native flora of the region. Flowers mid-April to July.

RED-OSIER DOGWOOD
Cornus stolonifera • Dogwood family: *Cornaceae*

■**DESCRIPTION** Red-osier dogwood is a mid-size deciduous shrub to 5 m in height. Its small white flowers (4 mm across) are grouped together to form dense round clusters approximately 10 cm across. By August they have been replaced by bunches of dull white inedible berries to 8 mm across. The leaves are typically dogwood: opposite, to 10 cm long, with parallel veins. Younger branches are pliable and have an attractive red colour.

■**HABITAT** Moist to wet areas, usually forested, at low to mid elevations.

■**NATIVE USE** The small branches were used for weaving, barbecue racks, fuel for smoking salmon and latticework for fishing weirs.

■**LOCAL SITES** Common; large patches on Cabbage and North Pender islands. Flowers late May. Fruit ripens beginning of August.

FALSEBOX or MOUNTAIN LOVER
Pachistima myrsinites • Staff tree family: *Celastraceae*

■ **DESCRIPTION** Falsebox is a small evergreen shrub to 75 cm in height. Its tiny maroon flowers go unnoticed by all but a curious few. The evergreen leaves are elliptic, leathery, tooth-edged, to 3 cm long. Falsebox is an attractive bush more noticed for its foliage than its flowers. The species name *myrsinites* is Greek for myrrh, in reference to the fragrant flowers.

■ **HABITAT** Forested mountain slopes at low to mid elevations. Rare on the coast, but abundant in the B.C. interior.

■ **LOCAL SITES** Common; large 2-m-wide specimens can be seen at Deep Bay and Mount Gibraltar on Jedediah Island. Flowering starts in April.

MOCK ORANGE

Philadelphus lewisii • Hydrangea family: *Hydrangeaceae*

■DESCRIPTION In flower, mock orange is a showy deciduous bush to 4 m in height. Its fragrant 4-petalled flowers are white with a yellow centre and grow to 3 cm across. The leaves are similar to the cultivated varieties, opposite, to 5 cm long, with 3 prominent veins. As the common name suggests, the flowers resemble orange blossoms.

144

■HABITAT Moist forested sites, at low to mid elevations.

■NATIVE USE The hard straight wood was used for arrows, pipe stems, fish spears and combs.

■LOCAL SITES Common on the Gulf Islands; large specimens trailside from Shingle Spit to Ford Cove on Hornby Island. Flowers May to July; the air is filled with perfume until June.

DOUGLAS MAPLE

Acer glabrum • Maple family: *Aceraceae*

■**DESCRIPTION** Douglas maple is a small deciduous tree to 10 m in height. Its long, palmate leaves are opposite, 5-10 cm across, and have 3-5 sharp lobes. The leaves of the closely related vine maple (*A. circinatum*) have 7-9 lobes. The pairs of winged seeds, or samaras, grow to 5 cm across and are joined at right angles.

■**HABITAT** Dry open forested sites, at low to mid elevations.

■**NATIVE USE** The hard, durable wood was used in many ways, including for snowshoe frames, drum hoops, tongs, throwing sticks, bows and masks.

■**LOCAL SITES** Common; large trees on Portland Island and in Helliwell Provincial Park on Hornby Island.

BIGLEAF MAPLE

Acer macrophyllum • Maple family: *Aceraceae*

■DESCRIPTION The bigleaf maple is the largest native maple on the West Coast, often exceeding heights of 30 m. Its huge leaves, which are dark green, 5-lobed, 20-30 cm across, are excellent identifiers. In early spring it produces beautiful clusters of scented yellow-green flowers, 7-10 cm long. The mature winged seeds (samaras), 5 cm long, act as whirlygigs when they fall; they are bountiful and an important food source for birds, squirrels, mice and chipmunks. The brown fissured bark is host to an incredible number of epiphytes, most commonly mosses and licorice ferns (see page 106).

■HABITAT Dominant in lower forested areas. Its shallow root system prefers moist soils, mild winters and cool summers.

■NATIVE USE The plentiful wood was important in native culture, as a fuel and for carvings, paddles, combs, fish lures, dishes and handles. The large leaves were used to line berry baskets and steam pits.

■LOCAL SITES Large specimens are common on the islands. Some of the biggest, over 2 m in diameter, can be found on Jedediah Island.

RED ALDER
Alnus rubra • Birch family: *Betulaceae*

■DESCRIPTION The largest native alder in North America, the red alder grows quickly and can reach 25 m in height. Its leaves are oval-shaped, grass green, 7-15 cm long, with a coarsely serrated edge. Hanging male catkins, 7-15 cm long, decorate the bare trees in early spring. The fruit (cones) are 1.5-2.5 cm long; they start off green, then turn brown and persist through winter. The bark is thin and grey on younger trees, scaly when older. Red alder leaves give a poor colour display in autumn, mainly green or brown.

■HABITAT Moist wooded areas, disturbed sites and stream banks at low to mid elevations.

■NATIVE USE The soft straight-grained wood is easily worked and was used for making masks, bowls, rattles, paddles and spoons. The red bark was used to dye fishnets, buckskins and basket material.

■LOCAL SITES Large straight-trunked specimens to 1 m in diameter can be seen on Orcas, Jedediah, Hornby and Newcastle islands.

PAPER BIRCH or CANOE BIRCH
Betula papyrifera • Birch family: *Betulaceae*

■**DESCRIPTION** Paper birch is a medium-size tree reaching heights of 20 m. Its serrated leaves are 8-12 cm long, rounded at the bottom and sharply pointed at the apex. Male and female catkins can be seen in early spring just before the leaves appear. The white peeling bark is a good identifier on younger trees. There is a red-bark variety that can be confused with the native bitter cherry (*Prunus emarginata*). The species name *papyrifera* means "to bear paper."

■**HABITAT** Rare in low-elevation coastal forests, common in interior forests; prefers moist soil and will tolerate wet sites.

■**NATIVE USE** The bark was used to make canoes, cradles, food containers, writing paper and coverings for teepees. The straight-grained wood was used for arrows, spears, snowshoes, sleds and masks.

■**LOCAL SITES** Not common; found on San Juan, Orcas, Galiano and Samuel islands.

151

ARBUTUS or PACIFIC MADRONE
Arbutus menziesii • Heather family: *Ericaceae*

■DESCRIPTION The arbutus is often seen as a contorted shrub or small tree, but in ideal conditions it can attain heights of 30 m. Its rhododendron-like leaves are leathery, glossy dark green above, silvery white below, to 15 cm long. The panicles of white flowers produced in spring are followed by clusters of orange-red berries 1 cm across. The reddish brown bark peels away every year to reveal a greenish underbark; the beautiful colours of the thin peeling outer bark are the key identifiers. The arbutus is Canada's only native broadleaf evergreen tree.

■HABITAT Dry coastal forests on the Gulf Islands, southeastern Vancouver Island and the adjacent coast. Southwestern B.C. is the northern extent of its range.

■NATIVE USE The leaves and bark were steeped as tea and used to cure colds and stomach aches. The wood cracks very easily and was rarely used to make tools or carvings.

■LOCAL SITES Common; its northern range is Denman, Hornby and Savory islands. Huge specimens are found at Montague Harbour on Galiano Island, Madrona Point on Orcas Island and on Waldron Island.

PACIFIC DOGWOOD

Cornus nuttallii • Dogwood family: *Cornaceae*

■DESCRIPTION Pacific dogwood ranges from being a multi-trunked shrub to a medium-size tree as tall as 19 m. Its leaves are elliptical, deep green above, lighter green below, to 10 cm long. The flowers are not quite as they seem: the 4-7 showy white petals are actually bracts that surround small, greenish white flowers. Clusters of small red berries 1 cm across appear by late summer. The bark is dark brown and smooth on young trees, scaly and ridged on older ones. The flower is the floral emblem of B.C., and the tree is protected by law. The painter and ornithologist John James Audubon named this tree after his friend Thomas Nuttall, the first person to classify it as a new species.

■HABITAT Coastal forests at low elevations.

■NATIVE USE The hard wood was used to make bows, arrows, harpoon shafts and, more recently, knitting needles.

■LOCAL SITES Less common on the San Juan Islands; recorded on most of the larger Gulf Islands. Flowering starts in mid-April; there is often a second smaller show in September.

CASCARA

Rhamnus purshiana • Buckthorn family: *Rhamnaceae*

■DESCRIPTION Cascara can be a multi-trunked shrub or a small tree to 9 m in height. Its leaves are oblong with prominent veins, glossy, grass green, 7-13 cm long. The flowers are small, greenish yellow and rather insignificant. The berries look like small cherries, 1-8 mm across, red at first, turning bluish black in late summer. The smooth bark is silvery grey and on older trees it resembles an elephant's hide. The bark was collected commercially for years and used as the key ingredient in laxatives.

■HABITAT Prefers moist, nutrient-rich sites in the shade of larger trees at low elevations.

■NATIVE USE The bark was boiled and the infusion used as a laxative.

■LOCAL SITES Rare on San Juan Islands, but large specimens can be found on Hornby, Jedediah and Portland islands.

PACIFIC CRAB APPLE

Malus fusca • Rose family: *Rosaceae*

■**DESCRIPTION** Pacific crab apple is a deciduous shrub or small tree 2-10 m high. Its leaves (5-10 cm long) are similar to those of orchard apple trees, except that they often have bottom lobes. The flowers are typical apple blossoms, white to pink, fragrant and in clusters of 5-12. The fruit that follows is 1-2 cm across, green at first, turning yellowy reddish. On older trees the bark is scaly and deeply fissured. The Pacific crab apple is B.C.'s only native apple.

■**HABITAT** High beaches, moist open forests, swamps and stream banks at lower elevations.

■**NATIVE USE** The small apples were an important food source, and the hard wood was used to make digging sticks, bows, handles and halibut hooks.

■**LOCAL SITES** Common; flowers end of April to May.

COTTONWOOD

Populus balsamifera ssp. *trichocarpa* •
Willow family: *Salicaceae*

■**DESCRIPTION** Cottonwood is the tallest deciduous tree in the Pacific Northwest. It is also one of the fastest-growing, attaining heights of 45 m and trunk diameters of 2-3 m. Its leaves are heart-shaped, alternating, dark shiny green above, pale green below, 7-15 cm long. The tiny seeds on female trees hang on 7- to 13-cm catkins and are covered in white fluffy hairs known as "cotton." The deeply furrowed bark and large sticky buds are good identifiers in winter. In early summer, bits of cotton can be seen filling the skies, transporting the seeds many kilometres away from the parent trees. The wood is used commercially to make tissue paper.

■**HABITAT** Low moist to wet areas across B.C. and Washington. Requires sunshine and will not tolerate heavy shade.

■**NATIVE USE** The sticky gum from the buds was boiled and used to stick feathers on arrow shafts and to waterproof baskets and birchbark canoes.

■**LOCAL SITES** More common on the larger Gulf Islands; large specimens at Tribune Bay on Hornby Island.

TREMBLING ASPEN
Populus tremuloides • Willow family: *Salicaceae*

■ **DESCRIPTION** Trembling aspen is a slender, deciduous tree to 25 m in height. Its small heart-shaped leaves are finely toothed and grow to 8 cm long; the leaf stalks are long and flattened, which is why the leaves tremble in the slightest breeze. Trembling aspens are dioecious.

■ **HABITAT** Damp soils in open sites and forests at low to mid elevations.

■ **NATIVE USE** The wood was used for small dugout canoes, tent poles and drying racks.

■ **LOCAL SITES** Small pure stands on Cabbage Island and at Oaks Bluff on North Pender Island, and several stands on North Galiano Island.

WILLOWS
Salix sp. • Willow family: *Salicaceae*

■DESCRIPTION Native willows are easy to identify as a genus but hard to distinguish as species. This is due to the variable leaf shapes within the same species, male and female flowers on separate plants, flowering before leaves appear and hybridization between species. The two most common willows are:

Scouler's willow (*Salix scouleriana*) – a shrub or tree 5-12 m in height, leaves 5-8 cm long, felty, narrow at the base and rounded at the tip. The flowers appear before the leaves, males to 4 cm long, females to 6 cm.

Pacific willow (*Salix lucida* ssp. *lasiandra*) – a shrub or tree 6-12 m in height, leaves 10-15 cm long, lance-shaped, with finely toothed edges. The flower appears with the leaves, males to 7 cm long, females to 12 cm.

■HABITAT Scattered in disturbed spots in young forests at low to mid elevations.

■LOCAL SITES Both species are common on the islands.

Scouler's Willow

Pacific Willow

< *Pacific Willow*

BLACK HAWTHORN
Crataegus douglasii • Rose family: *Rosaceae*

■DESCRIPTION Black hawthorn is an armed, scraggly shrub or bushy tree to 9 m in height. The leaves are roughly oval, coarsely toothed above the middle to 6 cm long. The clusters of white flowers are showy but bland in smell. The edible fruit is purple black to 1 cm long and hangs in bunches. Older bark is grey, patchy and very rough.

■HABITAT Prefers moist soil beside streams, in open forests or near the ocean.

163

■NATIVE USE The 3-cm thorns were used as tines on herring rakes.

■LOCAL SITES Less common on the San Juan Islands; wonderful old specimens between Whaling Station Bay and Cap Gurney on Hornby Island and at Coon Bay on Galiano Island; common on Gabriola Island. Flowers in May. Berries ripen by mid-July.

BITTER CHERRY
Prunus emarginata • Rose family: *Rosaceae*

■DESCRIPTION Bitter cherry is a small to medium-size tree, 5-15 m in height. Its bark is very distinctive: reddish brown with orange slits (lenticels), it is thin, smooth and peels horizontally. The white flowers (1 cm across) put on a wonderful show in April. The immature green fruit, 1 cm across, appear in early June and are bright red by midsummer. The leaves are quite different from those of the familiar Japanese cherries; they are alternate, 3-8 cm long, very finely toothed and usually rounded at the tip. The cherries are extremely bitter and considered inedible to humans, but are an important food source for birds. The fruit pits do not break down when digested, so birds carry them many kilometres from the parent tree.

■HABITAT Scattered in disturbed forests at low to mid elevations.

■NATIVE USE The shiny red bark was used to make baskets, mats and bags. The hard wood makes excellent fuel.

■LOCAL SITES Common forest tree; good representations on Gabriola, Saltspring and Galiano islands. Large specimens between Sylva Bay and Drumbeg Provincial Park on Gabriola Island. Flowers end of April to May.

GARRY OAK
Quercus garryana • Beech family: *Fagaceae*

■**DESCRIPTION** Even when stunted or windblown, Garry oak is the islands' stateliest deciduous tree. It ranges from 3 to 25 m in height; the male and female flowers are borne separately, but on the same tree. Like those of most white oaks, the leaves of the Garry oak are deeply round-lobed, to 12 cm long (red or black oaks have pointed lobes). The acorns are 2 cm long, with a bumpy cap. The light grey bark is tough, with thick ridges. David Douglas dedicated this tree to his friend Nicholas Garry, deputy governor of the Hudson's Bay Company.

■**HABITAT** Dry slopes and meadows on southeastern Vancouver Island, Gulf and San Juan islands and elsewhere in Washington State.

■**NATIVE USE** The acorns were eaten raw, boiled or roasted. The hard wood was used to make small tools.

■**LOCAL SITES** Common; Newcastle and Protection islands have some wonderful old leaning specimens. Hornby Island is home to the largest grove of ancient Garry oaks in B.C. The acorns ripen August through October.

WESTERN YEW or PACIFIC YEW
Taxus brevifolia • Yew family: *Taxaceae*

■**DESCRIPTION** Western yew is a small conifer from 3 to 15 m in height. It is usually seen as a straggly shrub or small tree in the understory of larger trees. Its thin brownish bark is scale-like, exposing reddish purple patches that distinguish it from the European species. Female trees produce a beautiful but poisonous red berry that ripens in August/September. The flat needles are 2-3 cm long, dark green above with white bands below. The cancer-fighting drug Taxol is extracted from yew bark.

CAUTION: the berries are considered poisonous.

■**HABITAT** Found intermittently on a variety of forested sites at low to mid elevations.

■**NATIVE USE** Western yew was considered the best wood for making bows.

■**LOCAL SITES** Commonly seen under 5 m on the Gulf Islands; Jedediah Island has some very old specimens. The tallest yew in B.C. is 22.25 m and is found at Fulford Harbour on Saltspring Island.

GRAND FIR

Abies grandis • Pine family: *Pinaceae*

■DESCRIPTION Grand fir is a remarkably fast-growing conifer that reaches heights of over 90 m. Its bark is thin and blistery on young trees, roughened into oblong plates divided by shallow fissures on older ones. The cones are erect, cylindrical, to 10 cm long and green to brown. The needles are dark green and flat, 2-4 cm long, grooved on top, with two white bands of stomata below. This is the tallest of the true firs and was aptly named "grand" by the botanist and explorer David Douglas.

■HABITAT A low-elevation species on the southern coast, most commonly found in moist areas where it grows with Douglas fir and western red cedar.

■NATIVE USE The wood was used as a fuel and to make canoes, fishhooks and hand tools. The boughs were brought inside as an air purifier.

■LOCAL SITES Common on the larger Gulf Islands; large specimens at Point Colville on Lopez Island, Friday Harbor on San Juan Island and Jedediah Island.

Picea sitchensis • Pine family: *Pinaceae*

CONIFERS

■DESCRIPTION Sitka spruce is often seen on rocky outcrops as a twisted dwarf tree, though in favourable conditions it can exceed 90 m in height. Its reddish brown bark is thin and patchy, a good identifier when the branches are too high to observe. The cones are gold brown, to 8 cm long. The needles are dark green, to 3 cm long and sharp to touch. Sitka spruce has the highest strength-to-weight ratio of any B.C. or Washington tree. It was used to build the frame of Howard Hughes' infamous plane *Spruce Goose*.

■HABITAT A temperate rainforest tree that does not grow farther than 200 km from the ocean.

■NATIVE USE The new shoots and inner bark were a good source of vitamin C. The best baskets and hats were woven from spruce roots, and the pitch (sap) was often chewed as a gum.

■LOCAL SITES Patchy on the larger islands.

SHORE PINE

Pinus contorta var. *contorta* • Pine family: *Pinaceae*

■DESCRIPTION Depending on where they are growing, shore pines vary dramatically in size and shape. By the shoreline they are usually stunted and twisted from harsh winds and nutrient-deficient soil. A little farther inland they can be straight-trunked to 20 m in height. The small cones, 3-5 cm long, are often slightly lopsided and remain on the tree for many years. The dark green needles are 4-7 cm long and grow in bundles of two. The nuts are edible but small and hard to reach. Another variety, lodgepole pine (*P. contorta* var. *latifolia*), grows straighter and taller, to 40 m.

■HABITAT The coastal variety grows in the driest and wettest sites, from low to high elevations.

■NATIVE USE The straight wood was used for teepee poles, torches and arrow and harpoon shafts.

■LOCAL SITES Common; forms dense stands on the San Juan Islands; beautiful windswept trees on Isle de Lis; large old specimens on Discovery Island.

DOUGLAS FIR
Pseudotsuga menziesii • Pine family: *Pinaceae*

■DESCRIPTION Douglas fir is a tall, fast-growing conifer to 90 m in height. Its bark is thick, corky and deeply furrowed. The ovate cones are 7-10 cm long and have 3 forked bracts protruding from the scales; the cones hang down from the branches, unlike true firs' cones, which stand up. The needles are 2-3 cm long, pointed at the apex, with a slight groove on the top and two white bands of stomata on the underside. The common name commemorates the botanist and explorer David Douglas.

■HABITAT Can tolerate dry to moist conditions from low to high elevations. Reaches its tallest size near the coast.

■NATIVE USE The wood was used for teepee poles, smoking racks, spear shafts, fishhooks and firewood.

■LOCAL SITES This is the dominant conifer on the Gulf Islands. Jedediah Island has some over 2 m in diameter; Moran and Jones state parks have some magnificent old groves. Even the tiny exposed island of Isle de Lis has some stunning windswept specimens.

WESTERN HEMLOCK
Tsuga heterophylla • Pine family: *Pinaceae*

■DESCRIPTION Western hemlock is a fast-growing pyramidal conifer to 60 m in height. Its reddish brown bark becomes thick and deeply furrowed on mature trees. The plentiful cones are small (2-2.5 cm long), conical and reddish when young. The flat, light green leaves vary in size from 0.5 to 2 cm long. The main leaders and new shoots are nodding, giving the tree a soft, pendulous appearance that is good for identification. Western hemlock is the state tree of Washington.

■HABITAT Flourishes on the Pacific coast from Alaska to Oregon and from low levels to 1,000 m, where it is replaced by mountain hemlock (*T. mertensiana*).

■NATIVE USE The wood has long been used for spear shafts, spoons, dishes, roasting spits and ridgepoles. The bark was boiled to make a red dye for wool and basket material.

■LOCAL SITES A common shade conifer on the islands.

WESTERN RED CEDAR
Thuja plicata • Cypress family: *Cupressaceae*

■DESCRIPTION Western red cedar is a large, fast-growing conifer with heights exceeding 60 m. Its bark sheds vertically and ranges from cinnamon red on young trees to grey on mature ones. The bases of older trees are usually heavily flared, with deep furrows. The egg-shaped cones are 1 cm long, green when young, turning brown and upright when mature (yellow cypress has round cones). The bright green leaves are scale-like, with an overlapping-shingle appearance.

Western red cedar is B.C.'s provincial tree. On old stumps, springboard marks can be seen 2-3 m above the ground; these allowed early fallers to get away from the flared bases. The shingle industry is now the biggest user of red cedar.

■HABITAT Thrives on moist ground at low elevations. Will tolerate drier or higher sites but will not attain gigantic proportions.

■NATIVE USE First Nations people know this tree as "the tree of life." It supplied them from birth to death, from cradle to coffin. The wood was used to make dugout canoes, fishing floats, paddles, bowls, masks, totem poles, ornamental boxes and spear and arrow shafts. The bark was shredded for clothing, diapers, mats, blankets, baskets and medicine.

■LOCAL SITES Common on the Gulf Islands; large 2-m-diameter specimens on Jedediah Island.

ROCKY MOUNTAIN JUNIPER

Juniperus scopulorum • Cypress family: *Cupressaceae*

■DESCRIPTION Rocky mountain juniper is usually seen as a shrub, but on occasion can form a beautiful weathered tree to 9 m in height. The bluish green leaves are in two forms: the juvenile growth is prickly, while the mature growth is softer and resembles the leaves of the western red cedar (*Thuja plicata*; see page 179). The reddish brown bark is thin and stringy, also like that of the red cedar. The trees are dioecious; the soft blue female cones are knobby, to 0.7 cm across, and grow in abundance.

■HABITAT Dry exposed sites.

■NATIVE USE Juniper wood was considered one of the best for making bows. The branches were burned as an incense and fumigant.

■LOCAL SITES Common on the Gulf Islands; Pirate's Cove on De Courcy Island has straight trees to 9 m in height.

Achene	A small, dry, one-seeded fruit (e.g., sunflower seeds).
Anther	The pollen-bearing (top) portion of the stamen.
Axil	The angle made between a stalk and a stem on which it is growing.
Biennial	Completing its life cycle in two growing seasons.
Bloom	A fine, powdery covering on stems, leaves or fruit.
Boss	Knob-like studs, as in the points on cones of yellow cypress.
Bract	A modified leaf below the flower.
Calyx	The collective term for sepals, the outer part of the flower.
Catkin	A spike-like or drooping flower cluster, male or female (e.g., cottonwood).
Corm	An underground swollen stem capable of producing roots, leaves and flowers.
Deciduous	A plant that sheds its leaves annually, usually in the autumn.
Dioecious	Male and female flowers on separate plants.
Epiphyte	A plant that grows on another plant for physical support, without robbing the host of nutrients.
Herbaceous perennial	A nonwoody plant that dies back to the ground each year and regrows the following season.
Lenticel	Raised organs that replace stomata on a stem.
Node	The place on a stem where the leaves and auxiliary buds are attached.
Obovate	Oval in shape, with the narrower end pointing downward, like an upside down egg.
Panicle	A branched inflorescence.

Pinnate	A compound leaf with the leaflets arranged on both sides of a central axis.
Pinnule	Leaflet of a pinnately compound leaf.
Raceme	Short-stalked flowers attached to a long, central stem (inflorescence).
Rhizome	An underground modified stem. Runners and stolons are on top of the ground.
Saprophyte	A plant that lives on dead or decaying matter.
Scape	A leafless stem rising from the ground. It may support one or many flowers.
Sepal	The outer parts of a flower, usually green.
Sori	Spore cases.

183

Stipe	Stalk (petiole), usually referring to ferns.
Stolon	A stem or branch that runs along the surface of the ground and takes root at the nodes or apex, forming new plants.
Stomata	The pores in the epidermis of leaves, usually seen as white.
Style	The stem of the pistil (female organ).
Tepal	A term used when there is no distinction between the sepals and petals.
Umbel	An inflorescence in which the stalks originate from a common point, like an umbrella.

Plant Parts   **Leaf Shapes**

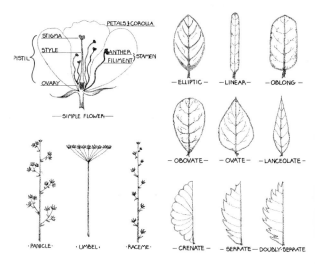

Adolph, Val. *Tales of the Trees*. Key Books, Delta, B.C., 2000

Atkinson, Scott and Sharpe, Fred. *Wild Plants of the San Juan Islands*. The Mountaineers, Seattle, Washington, 1993

Clark, Lewis J. *Wild Flowers of British Columbia*. Gray's Publishing Ltd., Sidney, B.C., 1973

Craighead, John J., Frank C. Craighead, Jr., and Ray J. Davis. *A Field Guide to Rocky Mountain Wildflowers*. Houghton Mifflin Company, Boston, Massachusetts, 1963

Haskin, L. L. *Wild Flowers of the Pacific Coast*. Binford and Mort, Portland, Oregon, 1934 (republished 1977, Dover Publications, New York)

Hitchcock, C. L., A. Cronquist, M. Ownbey, and J.W. Thompson. *Vascular Plants of the Pacific Northwest*. 5 pts. University of Washington Press, Seattle, Washington, 1955, 1959, 1961, 1964, 1969

Lyons, C. P. *Trees, Shrubs and Flowers to Know in British Columbia*. J. M. Dent and Sons, Toronto, Ontario and Vancouver, B.C., 1976 (1st ed. 1952)

Pojar, Jim, and MacKinnon, Andy. *Plants of the Pacific Northwest Coast*. Lone Pine Publishing, Vancouver, B.C., 1994

Sargent, Charles Sprague. *Manual of the Trees of North America*. 2 vols. Dover Publications, New York, 1965, two volumes (originally published in 1905 by Houghton Mifflin Company, Boston, Massachusetts)

Smith, Kathleen M. and Nancy J. Anderson. *Native West Coast As Seen in Lighthouse Park*. Sono Nis Press, Victoria, B.C., 1988

Stoltmann, Randy. *Hiking Guide to the Big Trees of Southwestern British Columbia*. Western Canada Wilderness Committee, Vancouver, B.C., 1987

Turner, Nancy J. *Plant Technology of First Peoples in British Columbia*. UBC Press, Vancouver, B.C., 1998

Turner, Nancy J. *Food Plants of Coastal First Peoples*. UBC Press, Vancouver, B.C., 2000

185

VALDES IS.

DIONISIO POINT

GALIANO IS.

WALLACE IS.

GULF ISLANDS

MONTAGUE HARBOUR
MARINE PARK

MAYNE IS.

CAMPBELL PT.

THETIS IS.

KUPER IS.

SECRETARY IS.

CHEMAINUS

CROFTON

SALTSPRING IS.

BAYNES PK.
1931'

BRUCE PK. 2306'

PREVOST IS.